A pug rides piggyback as a bulldog walks the red carpet at a pet festival in China.

125
True Stories of
Amazing
Animals

**NATIONAL
GEOGRAPHIC**

WASHINGTON, D.C.

Contents

Following the Herd
Page 90

Introduction

Welcome to the wonderful, hilarious, and heartwarming world of amazing animals.
Paw through these pages and find 125 of National Geographic Kids' favorite true tales of animal friendships, animal heroes, amazing pet tricks, animal intelligence, and more! Meet Tonda, the orangutan who takes her pet cat T.K. everywhere with her. Check out a glamorous guinea pig named Fuzzberta with her own fan following. And go globe-trotting with Oscar, likely the most well traveled terrier on Earth. He has been photographed at landmarks across the globe from Italy to India to Costa Rica, including posing nose to nose with the Sphinx statue in Egypt. These wacky stories are not only fun to read, they may also push the limits of what humans think animals can do. So let the fur fly, and join this zany parade of amazing animals.

A parrot shows that he's no lightweight at a bird park in Wuhan, China.

Bailey Jr. the bison isn't a backseat driver. He doesn't fit! His owner, Jim Sautner, removed the car's roof and passenger seats, and reinforced the floorboards so Bailey Jr. could ride around town with him and Charlie Brown the cocker spaniel. See page 37 for Jim's other bison pet.

DOG RESCUES 200 CATS!

Wuffy relaxes with Mao Mao the cat.

Wuffy hangs out with Buttercup (above) and Simone (right).

LOS ANGELES, CALIFORNIA, U.S.A.

Wuffy the dog is always on the lookout for cats. But she doesn't chase or bark at them. She rescues them.

Eleven years ago, owner Gary Rohde was shocked when Wuffy popped out of some bushes with a weak kitten in her mouth. Then she brought out three more! Back home, Wuffy cared for them like a mother cat, licking their faces. "They were drenched with dog spit," Rohde says. Thanks to Wuffy, the kittens survived.

Since then, Wuffy has rescued more than 200 cats. She's even on call with a local rescue group, which sends her troubled cats that need attention, such as Mao Mao. He hissed and spit so much that rescuers worried no one would want to adopt him. Wuffy shared her sleeping space with Mao Mao, cuddled with him, and taught him to trust new friends. Now the cat has a home of his own.

Why does Wuffy favor felines? That mystery hasn't been solved. "I didn't teach her how to do it," Rohde says. "Even her veterinarian is stumped."

TWO-HEADED SNAKE

ST. LOUIS, MISSOURI, U.S.A.

The albino black rat snake fittingly named We never gets any privacy. But there's not another snake crowding her space—it's her other head!

We's heads are actually twins from two eggs that grew together. That's unusual, but this snake is full of surprises. We is a "she" on her bottom half, but differences in size and skin patterns show that one head is female and the other is male. The two don't realize they're connected. "If they did, one would smack the other and say, 'Let go of me!'" says Leonard Sonnenschein, president of the World Aquarium where We lives.

Most two-headed snakes live only a few months, but seven-year-old We has gotten special care at the aquarium. One thing's for sure: She definitely won't ever be lonely!

A black rat snake can grow nearly 8 1/2 feet long, making it one of the longest snakes in North America.

ELEPHANTS
STEAL SNACK!

CHACHOENGSAO PROVINCE, THAILAND

Getting a flat tire is bad enough. But sneaky elephants ambushing your tapioca-filled delivery truck is a disaster! The driver of the truck had gone to find help for his flat tire. When he returned, a group of elephants had surrounded his vehicle and were devouring his load! One was even carrying in its trunk the tarp that had covered the tapioca—a sure sign that the elephants used their brainpower to get to their snack. The army was called in, but there was no need: As soon as the elephants ate their fill, they left. Maybe they were hoping to find an ice-cream truck next!

Tapioca comes from the root of the cassava plant and can be used to make pudding.

HURRY! THE DRIVER WON'T BE GONE FOREVER!

11

FOX COLLECTS SHOES

FÖHREN, GERMANY

Who'd want someone else's stinky shoes? That's what residents of one town wondered when their shoes started vanishing from their doorsteps. Suspects included neighbors, dogs—even their own kids. Then a forest worker discovered close to 250 shoes scattered near a fox den. A fox had outfoxed the town!

Why would a four-legged furball want a pair of shoes? Like dogs, foxes enjoy chewing and playing. John Hadidian, director of urban wildlife programs for the Humane Society of the United States, thinks the fox was probably just having fun. But that doesn't mean all foxes are shoe thieves. "This is probably one fox out of millions," he says. "She has in her head that she likes shoes."

The recovered shoes were displayed in town so residents could reclaim their footwear. As for the fox, she's moved on to new territory—but the townspeople now know better than to leave their shoes outside.

Residents search the recovered stolen goods for their missing shoes.

BEAR HAS GIANT TONGUE

Sun bears have the longest tongues of any bear species.

ST. LOUIS, MISSOURI, U.S.A.

Rimba the Malayan sun bear reveals a shocking secret when he opens his mouth at the St. Louis Zoo. It's not bad breath—it's a foot-long tongue.

Rimba darts his tongue into logs to search for food. "We drill holes in tree logs and hide things like peanut butter and raisins," says mammal curator Steve Bircher. Rimba may look a little unusual, but in the wild sun bears need their long tongues to survive. Unlike other bears, who spend most of their time on the ground, sun bears hang out in trees. They cling to branches with their paws, and they use their tongues to lap up insects and honey.

You'd think such a long tongue might cause Rimba to trip, but he's actually quite graceful. "He likes to sit on a high branch and tie rope around himself," Bircher says. At least Rimba isn't tongue-tied!

Malayan sun bears live in the rain forests of Southeast Asia.

DOG SURVIVES CLIFF FALL

WATCH OUT, BIRD. YOU MAY HAVE LED ME OFF A CLIFF ONCE, BUT I'LL CATCH YOU NEXT TIME.

EAST SUSSEX, ENGLAND, U.K.

Poppy the English springer spaniel was just doing what she loved when she chased a seagull at a seaside park. But when the gull flapped away, Poppy kept chasing it—right over a 300-foot cliff!

Her horrified dog walkers rushed to the edge and looked down. Poppy had fallen straight into the English Channel. She was alive but helpless in the chilly waves.

As the humans called for help, the clever canine paddled to a tiny beach about 30 feet away. For ten minutes she huddled there until a rescue boat from the Royal National Lifeboat Institution reached the soaked-but-safe dog.

Spaniels are great swimmers, says Ginnie Klein of the Golden Gate English Springer Spaniel Association. But surviving such an ordeal is "pure dumb luck," she says. Poppy may wish she could fly as well as swim!

"It's *good* to be a ball hog!"

PIG ATHLETES

"Sure, we like to swim, but what's up with the hats?"

"Forget the finish line. We're headed for the buffet line!"

A pig's funny-looking snout helps the animal dig.

MOSCOW, RUSSIA

Now even pigs can have gold-medal dreams! During the third annual Pig Games last year, Russian pigs faced a fierce team of international competitors in sports such as pigball (like soccer), pig swimming, and pig racing.

Russia's sporting swine live in a special complex where vets and coaches keep them in fabulous form. Nariner Bagmanyan, whose company organizes the games, says the well-trained Russian pigs were calm and focused before their events. Or maybe they just had their eyes on the prize: a tub of cooked carrots with cream!

The home team left its challengers in the dust, winning all three events. Russia's pigball players defeated the international team by a whopping 16 to 3. But Bagmanyan cuts the visiting athletes some slack: "To play soccer in a foreign country is probably difficult for everybody, even pigs."

Guinea pigs aren't pigs but may have gotten their name from their squealing noises.

GUINEA PIG GETS GLAM

PACIFICA, CALIFORNIA, U.S.A.

Fuzzberta is a rescued guinea pig who—get this—has attracted a fan following for her adorable disguises and costumes. Her owner, "Monica the human," loves to snap the glamorous guinea pig in all kinds of silly scenarios—running from monsters, fighting dragons, going dogsledding, or even dressed as Einstein, complete with a tiny wig! Monica and Fuzzberta aim to spread happiness with their fantastic photos. When she's not in disguise, Fuzzberta loves snacking on strawberries or hanging out with her guinea pig pals: MiniGuineaPig, Jennifuzz, Billy Blob, Jelly Baby, and Shnoopy. But who knows where Fuzzberta will appear next—or what she'll appear as!

SWAN *LOVES* PADDLEBOAT

MÜNSTER, GERMANY

Schwarzer Peter the black swan is in love. Unfortunately, the bird doesn't seem to realize that the object of his affection is actually a paddleboat that just *looks* like a swan!

Schwarzer Peter hardly ever leaves his "sweetheart." He keeps a close eye on the boat when he's feeding and follows if someone tries to paddle it. Sailboaters know not to get too close to the white "swan": Schwarzer Peter noisily chases them away!

Is it true love? It may be a behavior called imprinting, in which a baby bird follows the first thing it sees, usually its parents. "So the paddleboat may just remind the swan of a large, white version of its parents," says swan expert William Sladen. Whether it's love or imprinting, the two remain inseparable. Peter Overschmidt, who runs a local sailing school, agrees: "They seem very happy together."

Black swans often give piggyback rides to their babies.

TALK ABOUT A DOG-AND-PONY SHOW.

DOG RIDES PONY

Newborn puppies are blind and deaf until they're about two weeks old.

GLOUCESTERSHIRE, ENGLAND, U.K.

"Giddyap!" That's the message Freddie the Jack Russell terrier seems to be giving Daisy the Shetland pony. The pair's favorite game is when the dog leaps onto the pony's back and goes for a ride. Their friendship started when Freddie spotted Daisy about to give a child a ride. Frantic to be included, the dog tore across the yard and leaped straight up. "He settled down right where the saddle would go," says the dog's owner, Patricia Swinley. "Daisy didn't seem to mind." From then on, the flop-eared equestrian rode Daisy two or three times a day. Says Swinley: "Freddie would do anything to be part of the party."

ORPHANED ELEPHANT TAKES CHARGE

NAIROBI, KENYA

When she was just a few weeks old, a small elephant sadly lost her mother to a poacher attack. Luckily, the little elephant was found by a farmer and taken to an elephant orphanage, where she was named Natumi. There, at the David Sheldrick Wildlife Trust in Nairobi, Kenya, Natumi was safe, but very scared and shy. Soon, however, new orphaned baby elephants began to arrive at the shelter. At first, Natumi hid behind her keepers' legs. But it soon became clear that the other baby elephants needed someone to depend on. They were very young, and many of them had injuries like sunburns and scratches. To everyone's surprise, shy little Natumi stepped up to the task. She began to act like a big sister to the seven other elephants, keeping them calm and playing with them in the surrounding bush. Soon, the elephants had formed their own loving family, thanks to Natumi's guidance. Eventually, the new family of elephants was strong and healthy enough to return to the wild—but the workers at the shelter would never forget a little elephant named Natumi who made it possible.

LITTLE OCTOPUS MAKES BIG MESS!

SANTA MONICA, CALIFORNIA, U.S.A.

Workers at an aquarium arrived one morning to a squishy mystery: Two inches of seawater covered the floor. After a lot of mopping and a little detective work, they discovered that the culprit was a mischievous two-spotted octopus.

Apparently the inquisitive octopus became curious about a tube that fed seawater into her tank. Wrapping an arm around it, she pushed and pulled until it popped out. Water gushed from the tube for six hours, flooding the floor with nearly 800 gallons of water. That's like pouring out 12,800 lunch-size cartons of milk.

"Octopuses are extremely intelligent and curious," says Santa Monica Pier Aquarium director Vicki Wawerchak. "In the wild, she'd be reaching into crevices and prying open shells." This octopus may have been too smart for her own good.

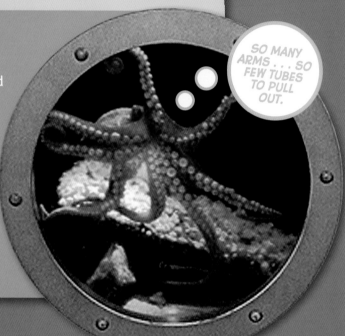

SO MANY ARMS . . . SO FEW TUBES TO PULL OUT.

Austin Forman gives his dog, Angel, a hug for saving his life.

DOG SAVES BEST FRIEND

BOSTON BAR, CANADA

Angel the golden retriever sensed danger in the backyard and stuck close to her owner, 11-year-old Austin Forman. Then the dog saw it: a cougar stalking the boy. Suddenly the wildcat lunged at Austin. Angel sprang into action, putting herself between the boy and the predator.

The cougar wrestled Angel to the ground and dragged her under a porch. Within three minutes, a nearby police officer had rescued Angel from the cougar's jaws. But the dog wasn't moving. Would she survive?

A moment later, Angel gasped for air. Then she jumped up, shook her fur, and looked for Austin. "Nothing could have stopped Angel from protecting Austin, even if it meant risking her life," says pet relationship expert Linda Anderson.

Except for a few scars, Angel completely recovered. Angel received a big steak—and lots of love—as thanks for saving her best friend's life.

6 SiLLY PEt TRiCKS

Just teaching a dog to sit can be a challenge, but these adventurous pets have been trained to perform some totally wild tricks. Check out these awesome animals in action!

THESE PETS LIKE DOING TRICKS, BUT YOUR PET MAY NOT. NEVER FORCE YOUR PET TO DO A TRICK IT DOES NOT WANT TO DO.

FORGET HANG 10— I'M HANGIN' 18 TOES, DUDE!

Surf's up for Curly!

1

Bunsen takes a surfing break on his radio-controlled boat.

MICE SHRED THE WAVES

COOMBABAH, QUEENSLAND, AUSTRALIA

Curly, Bunsen, and Harry the mice may be the world's smallest surfers. They shred three-foot-high waves tossed up by boats cruising along Australia's coast! The little squeakers were babies when owner Shane Willmott taught them to swim in the bathtub. Later, he pulled them around his pool on home-made miniature surfboards. Soon they hit the beach. "I push them onto a wave, and I'm right there to pick them up when they're done," Willmott says. And in case of a wipeout? He sometimes dyes the animals' fur so they're easy to spot. Out of the water, the rad rodents live in custom-built condos and gorge themselves on their favorite treat: toast soaked in melted butter and milk. Sweet!

Harry the mouse is learning to parasail.

The American Eskimo dog has no connection to the American Eskimo culture.

MYRTLE BEACH, SOUTH CAROLINA, U.S.A.

Don't tell Dick the American Eskimo dog he can't learn new tricks. He'll flip—literally! It took three years and countless boxes of dog treats, but now Dick turns more than five backward somersaults in a row. "When Dick was a puppy, he was very jumpy and always tried to reach high places," says owner Denis Ignatov. He began playing Frisbee with the dog, tossing the disk so that Dick had to jump and lean backward at the same time to catch it. Once Dick mastered that, the trainer used his hands to flip Dick all the way over. Soon the dog got so good that Ignatov stopped helping. But Dick didn't stop helping himself to the dog treats!

2 DOG TURNS FLIPS

3 FISH SCORES GOAL

GIBSONIA, PENNSYLVANIA, U.S.A.

He may not qualify for the World Cup, but Albert Einstein the calico fantail goldfish sure can handle a soccer ball. To train his fish to push the ball into a goal, owner Dean Pomerleau held a straw under the water and dropped food pellets through it. Eventually, the fish associated the straw's tip with food. Then Pomerleau placed a weighted-down miniature soccer ball and goal in Albert's tank and lured Albert to the ball with the straw. The fish would get treats when he touched the ball. Soon Albert was guiding it into the net. "Now when I put the ball and goal into the tank, he instantly swims up to the ball and starts pushing it in," Pomerleau says. Al doesn't need shin guards—but maybe he could use some "fin" guards!

Goldfish can live to be 20 years old.

4
PELICAN PLAYS CATCH

NEW SOUTH WALES, AUSTRALIA

Pong the Australian pelican can't hit a tennis ball, but she's great at catching one. Whenever trainer Allison Starr (above) throws a ball in the air, Pong stretches out her neck, opens her beak, and ... *plop*—she's got it! Pong then drops the ball into Starr's hand, and the fun continues. Starr discovered Pong's talent when the trainer absentmindedly tossed a leaf into the air. Pong reached out and snagged it, and the trick was born. "After playing awhile, she would stretch out her neck and rest it over my shoulder," Starr says. Then Pong would make a burping sound. Guess that's her way of saying, "Thanks for playing!"

Pong the pelican likes to snuggle.

5

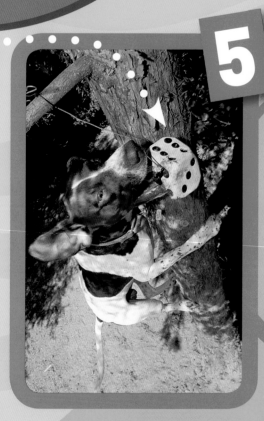

CATS JAM IN BAND

6

DOG CLIMBS TREE

MARTINEZ, CALIFORNIA, U.S.A.

Buster the German short-haired pointer is barking up the right tree—any tree—to retrieve his toys. After the playful pup scrambled up a redwood tree chasing a squirrel, owner Bob Wilhelm stuck the dog's tennis ball up in the branches. "I didn't know if he'd get the ball at all," Wilhelm says. But sure enough, Buster went for it. The powerful pooch gave himself a running start, took a flying leap, and dug his claws into the trunk's soft bark. Up and up he scooched until his head was eight feet off the ground. Then he knocked the ball down with his nose. Soon he retrieved all his toys the same way. Buster isn't just a tree climber—he's also a lifesaver. Buster alerted his owner's wife when her elderly mother suffered a heart attack.

German short-haired pointers have webbed feet.

CHICAGO, ILLINOIS, U.S.A.

Dakota, Darby, and Pinky the cats can't read music—but that doesn't stop them from playing it! With Dakota on drums, Darby on the keyboard, and Pinky on guitar, the tone-deaf band known as the Rock Cats entertains people with their "music"—even if the people have to cover their ears to listen. Owner Samantha Martin trained the group using a clicker. Every time the cats made a sound with their instruments, Martin clicked and gave out bites of chicken. "It didn't take them long to figure out that I was after the sound," she says. And Tuna, the backup guitarist, has another trick: After each performance, he taps a tip jar for the audience to drop cash into!

A white cat with blue eyes is more likely than other cats to be deaf.

YOU'VE GOT A LITTLE POND GOOP ON YOUR BEAK.

DUCK BEFRIENDS DOG

NEAR DES MOINES, IOWA, U.S.A.

A dog and a duck hanging out might "quack" you up, but that's just normal to best buds Sterling the duck and Cleo the Labrador retriever mix. Owner Tiffany Smith decided to introduce the unlikely friends after Sterling lost his duck pal. The two got off to a rocky start. "The dog didn't like the duck at first," Smith says. "But Sterling kept following her everywhere, and eventually Cleo got used to the duck being around." The pair spends most of the day playing in the pond and exploring the tall grasses in the backyard. When it's bedtime, they share a kennel. But rather than curling up in a corner, Sterling will rest his head on the dog's stomach as they snooze. They also share food. Sterling prefers dog chow over duck feed and sometimes eats out of Cleo's bowl. Says Smith, "It's the best relationship between animals I've ever seen."

Snack time! Sterling and Cleo share some kibble.

CAT MODELS ON CAMERA

Snoopy's parents were an American shorthair and a Persian cat.

CHENGDU, SICHUAN PROVINCE, CHINA

This may be the internet's most fashionable feline. Snoopybabe—or Snoopy for short—is an exotic shorthair cat who lives in China. Famous for his adorable flat face and enormous eyes, Snoopy is a model in many ways, from his unique look to his range of accessories. Snoopy has been photographed wearing hats, sweaters, socks, and even fancy necklaces. Maybe one day this ultracool kitty will be on a catwalk in *Mew*lan, Italy. Until then, he's sure to keep delighting his fans with his fashionable photographs.

HORSES BECOME MODELS

Where's the red carpet? Florence glams it up.

LONDON, ENGLAND, U.K.

These horses are ready for their close-ups. Florence the chestnut horse and several other equines were the stars of a funny photo shoot by Julian Wolkenstein. Hair stylist Acacio da Silva created horsey hairstyles ranging from curly movie star hairdos to colorfully beaded braids. The horses got model treatment: da Silva wove hair extensions into the horses' manes, then styled the dos with hair straighteners, rollers, and blow dryers. Eventually the horses' diva attitudes came out. "Every so often they'd wander away until we gave them an apple," Wolkenstein says. "I think they enjoyed the attention." Looks like the Next Top Model may have four legs and a mane!

Misty is one horn away from becoming a unicorn.

27

DOG INVENTS GAME!

OH BOY, OH BOY, OH BOY! DOWN I GO!

WATER. ROCKS. I AM EASILY AMUSED.

Springer spaniels were named for their ability to "spring" forward to drive birds out of hiding, back when the dogs were used primarily for hunting.

LYME REGIS, ENGLAND, U.K.

Bella the springer spaniel loves swimming, but she doesn't do just the dog paddle. As soon as she spies a lake or a river, she jumps in, disappears underwater, then pops out with a rock in her mouth! "The first time she did it, I thought I was going to have to go in and get her," says owner Rob Vaughan. "I was very surprised."

Other dogs can swim underwater, but they rarely invent a game out of it. Bella feels around the bottom of a lake or river with her paws until she finds the perfect rock. Then she plunges under until just her tail sticks out. "She's stayed under about 30 seconds getting a rock," Vaughan says. Bella even retrieves rocks Vaughan tosses into the water over and over. She's definitely earned her nickname: Aquadog!

PARROT SAVES FAMILY

MUNCIE, INDIANA, U.S.A.

Shannon Conwell woke to a piercing noise. Confused, he opened his eyes and saw thick, black smoke. The house was on fire! But the sound wasn't the smoke alarm. It was Peanut the parrot *imitating* the alarm, which his owner could barely hear. Conwell fled the house with his nine-year-old son, Tyler, and Peanut. "Within four minutes, the couch we were sleeping on was in flames," he says.

Before the fire, Conwell had heard Peanut say a few words and mimic the telephone. But he'd never heard Peanut sound the alarm. In fact, he's pretty sure the bird had never heard the smoke alarm until that night. One recent study found that parrots may not just mimic sounds—they might really understand what the sounds mean. "I believe he was trying to wake me up," Conwell says. "If it weren't for that bird, we would have been in big trouble."

YOU SHOULD HEAR MY IMITATION OF HANNAH MONTANA.

Some wild parrots eat clay to absorb toxins found in the seeds they eat.

WHAT DO YOU MEAN I'M NOT SUPPOSED TO LEAVE MY CAGE?

Like guide dogs that "see" for the blind, capuchins have been trained to be "hands" for people who can't move their upper bodies.

SMART MONKEY FOOLS KEEPERS

TUPELO, MISSISSIPPI, U.S.A.

Oliver the capuchin monkey is always acting naughty—screeching, running in circles, and tossing toys around his cage. But the monkey turned sneaky: Oliver waited till all the park workers went home, reached out of his cage, picked the lock, and escaped the zoo—twice!

Some keepers think he used his small fingers to pick the lock. As to why, you may want to ask his monkey girlfriend, Baby. "Oliver may have been trying to impress her," says park administrator Michelle Latham of the Tupelo Buffalo Park and Zoo. "He kind of shows off when she's around." Oliver likes Baby so much that keepers recorded her "talking" and played it over a loudspeaker to lure him back home. It worked!

Since the second escape, the zoo has added three more locks and installed two cameras to watch Oliver 24/7. Looks like he'll have to find a new way to wow his girlfriend.

DON'T WORRY— I DON'T EAT VERY MUCH.

RAT STEALS LEOPARD'S FOOD

HERTFORDSHIRE, ENGLAND, U.K.

This baby rat was either very brave, very hungry—or very stupid! During feeding time at a zoo, the rat scampered into Sheena the leopard's enclosure, snatched a piece of raw meat, and started snacking. Shocked onlookers thought the rodent was about to become an appetizer. But Sheena seemed to be the scaredy-cat. "When the rat moved, Sheena was startled and jumped away," photographer Casey Gutteridge says.

Sheena finally got up the nerve to lightly paw and sniff the rat. Then she went back to her meal, allowing the tiny thief to take what it wanted. It turns out the rat was never in danger. "Rats aren't normally prey for an adult leopard, and they don't pose any threat," says Joe Maynard of the Cat House, a feline conservation center. "A leopard would usually just ignore a rat." Or, in this case, invite it over for dinner!

Leopard nuzzles rat!

RABBIT JOINS HOSPITAL STAFF

Alyna is ready to roll!

JERUSALEM, ISRAEL

Calling Dr. Rabbit! When six-year-old Mussa, who has trouble walking, refused to wear his scary-looking leg braces, ALYN Hospital staff brought in Alyna the rabbit. The bunny, whose back legs don't work, wears braces, too. When Mussa saw a rabbit wearing braces, he wanted to as well. Now Mussa and the rabbit race the hospital hallways together—leg braces and all.

Alyna was born with her back legs paralyzed. So owner Riki Yahalom Arbel, who works at the hospital, fitted the rabbit with a miniature skateboard-like brace. The bunny pulls herself forward with her front legs while her back legs roll along.

Arbel figured Alyna's disability might help encourage patients who were mobility challenged. She was right. When kids like Mussa see how the rabbit moves, they want to wear their braces. "The kids take turns strapping Alyna onto her 'skateboard,' and she loves it," says Cathy Lanyard, executive director of the American Friends of ALYN Hospital. "She's like part of the staff—but she gets paid in unlimited snacks and plenty of hugs."

Mussa and Alyna help each other feel better.

BEAVER DAM VISIBLE FROM SPACE

DID WE BUILD THE DAM BIG ENOUGH TO PUT A HOT TUB INSIDE?

WOOD BUFFALO NATIONAL PARK, ALBERTA, CANADA

You've heard of busy beavers. But these guys take the phrase to a whole new level: They built a 2,800-foot-long dam, the longest known beaver dam on Earth. It's so big it can be seen from space!

The critters' construction zone is in a remote national park accessible only by helicopter, so no one even knew it existed until recently. Researcher Jean Thie accidentally discovered it while studying satellite photos for signs of climate change. Instead he spotted high water levels, dead trees, and lodges—sure signs of a dam.

The steady flow of water from the nearby mountains is a trigger that means the beavers will keep adding on to their dam. "When beavers hear water, they build," says research biologist Matt Peek. "They'll even build a dam on top of a tape recorder playing the sound of flowing water." That's something to chew on.

This satellite image shows the beaver dam inside the red outline.

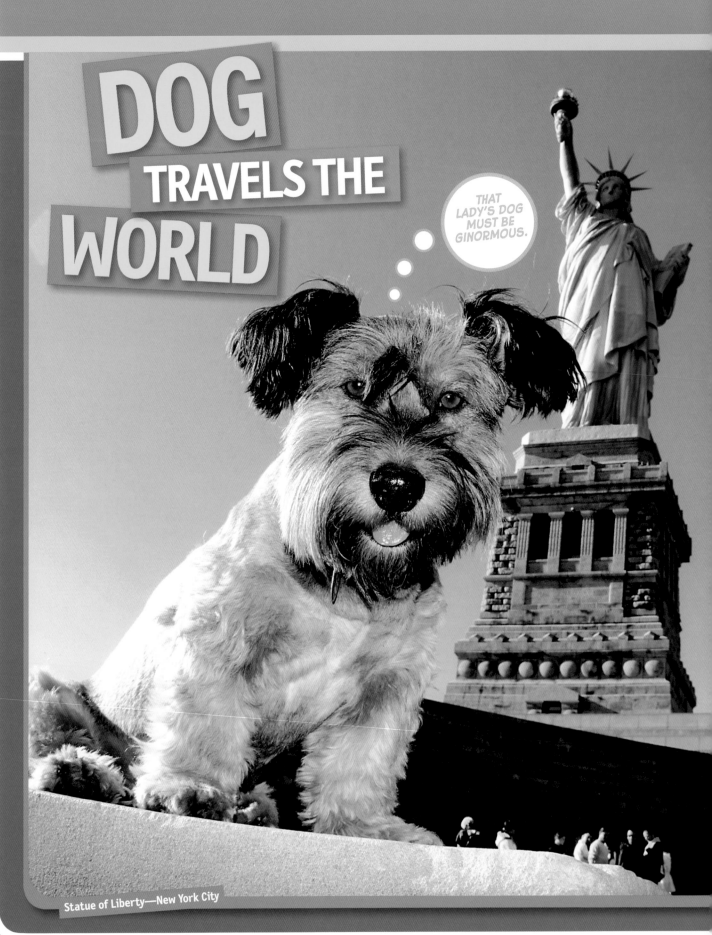

DOG TRAVELS THE WORLD

THAT LADY'S DOG MUST BE GINORMOUS.

Statue of Liberty—New York City

Leaning Tower of Pisa—Italy

WONDER WHAT'S HOLDING THAT THING UP?

WHAT'S WITH THE HUMPS ON THIS HORSE?

Camel-riding—India

OSCAR THE TERRIER MIX had already met monkeys in Nepal and llamas in Peru on his 'round-the-world trip. But nothing prepared him for one particular day in India. He not only met a camel—he also rode it through the desert!

Oscar wasn't just sightseeing. He and his owner, Joanne Lefson, were showing the world that you don't have to buy an expensive, pure-bred dog to find a good pet. "I wanted to show that great shelter dogs do exist," Lefson says.

Over eight-and-a-half months, Oscar rode trains to see the Colosseum in Rome, Italy, and the Eiffel Tower in Paris, France. He flew to Kenya, in Africa, to watch lions in the wild and to Egypt to sniff an ancient "lion"—the Sphinx statue. He floated down the Ganges River in India, where he also relaxed near the Taj Mahal. Oscar even zip-lined with Lefson through a Costa Rican rain forest.

Oscar and Lefson traveled about 46,000 miles—almost twice the circumference of the Earth—and visited 66 shelters to show that good pets like Oscar are available for adoption. "People kept asking where they could get a dog like him," she says.

What's next for Oscar? A lot of rest—and the best scrapbook ever.

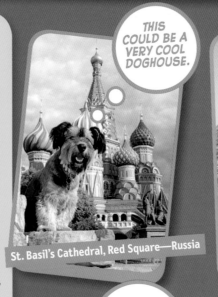
THIS COULD BE A VERY COOL DOGHOUSE.
St. Basil's Cathedral, Red Square—Russia

I THINK WE LOOK A LITTLE ALIKE, DON'T YOU?
The Sphinx—Egypt

I DON'T SEE WHY I HAVE TO WEAR THE BODYSUIT.
Zip-lining—Costa Rica

WHEW! GLOBE-TROTTING IS EXHAUSTING!
Taj Mahal—India

OTTER RIDES KAYAK!

ARE WE THERE YET?

An otter's nimble front paws can grab prey such as crawfish out from under rocks.

DÜSSELDORF, GERMANY

It's easy finding Nemo the otter. Just look for the kayak. Wolfgang Gettmann adopted Nemo after the otter's mother rejected him. One day the curious otter spotted Gettmann's red kayak and hopped right on board. Soon he joined his new dad for kayak journeys along local rivers.

Otters usually spend most of their time in the water, so Nemo is completely at home both on the kayak and in the river. "He goes back and forth between the boat and the water," Gettmann says. "He catches fish and brings them up on the kayak to eat."

Gettmann is like an adoptive father to Nemo, and the otter seems to have adopted Gettmann's kayaking friends as his family, too. The otter frequently hops aboard familiar kayaks and playfully nips the paddlers' hands. It's his way of saying, "hello"—or, perhaps, "paddle faster!"

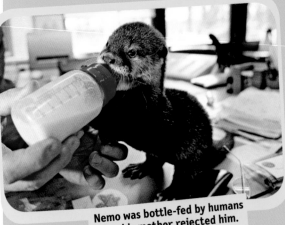
Nemo was bottle-fed by humans after his mother rejected him.

PENGUIN BECOMES
KNIGHT

EDINBURGH, SCOTLAND, U.K.

Sir Nils Olav is a king penguin, but he's not really a king, he's a knight. Since 1972 the Norwegian King's Guard—which protects Norway's royal family in times of crisis—has been "adopting" king penguins as mascots. One reason is that the birds' black-and-white feathers resemble the soldiers' uniforms. Over the years, Nils has been promoted from member, to sergeant major, to colonel in chief, and now to knight. "Nils instantly recognizes the soldiers when they visit," says penguin keeper Roslin Talbot. "He waddles over and squawks at them." His knighthood ceremony was no different. Before receiving a sword tap on each shoulder (top right), Nils walked past the line of soldiers at attention, occasionally stopping to inspect the troops. All the knighted penguin needs now is a suit of armor.

Centuries ago, knights worked for their king. Today knights are still appointed by the royal family, but the title is mostly symbolic and a reward for outstanding contributions to the country.

Norwegian soldiers visit Sir Nils every few years at his zoo home in Scotland.

NEXT TIME I WANT A VACATION I'LL GO ON A CRUISE.

LOST PARROT
GIVES ADDRESS

NAGAREYAMA, JAPAN

Yosuke the parrot is no birdbrain. He got lost once, and the African gray parrot was able to tell his rescuers his full name and exactly where he lived.

When Yosuke's owner took him outside for some fresh air, Yosuke flapped away. "We looked for Yosuke for three days, but we couldn't find him," Yoshio Nakamura says. "We thought he wouldn't come back."

What Nakamura didn't know was that police had found Yosuke and took him to a veterinarian. At first, Yosuke was shy. Then he started greeting people and singing. Suddenly, after about ten days, he squawked, "I'm Mr. Yosuke Nakamura," and recited his address.

African grays are known for their intelligence and vocabulary. Yosuke knows about 50 phrases and took about a month to learn his address. Good thing he did—getting lost is strictly for the birds.

Yosuke is pronounced YOH-soo-kay. His owner named him that because he wanted him to be a brilliant bird, and "yo" is Japanese for brilliant!

SEEING FOR TWO

VAN NUYS, CALIFORNIA, U.S.A.

Samson the Akita shepherd isn't an official Seeing Eye dog. That doesn't stop him from being a "guide dog" for his blind friend Delilah the Lhasa apso. When Barbara Fiero spotted the pair of strays wandering the highway, she noticed something strange: Samson (above, right) kept nudging Delilah away from oncoming traffic. After Fiero brought them to her house, she discovered that Delilah was blind. Samson had been leading Delilah as if he were her guide dog! Years later Samson still keeps Delilah in sight, checking on her constantly and standing guard when strangers are around. But he has mellowed a bit. "He lets Delilah sit by herself on the couch," Fiero says. "He just lies on a pillow nearby with his paws in the air."

SITTING BULL

EDMONTON, ALBERTA, CANADA

Bailey the bison has a home on the range—literally! The 1,600-pound North American bison actually hangs out in the house with his owners. Sure, Bailey eats, sleeps, and goes to the bathroom outside, but he also pays visits to his owners *inside*. Bailey was rejected by his mother, so Jim Sautner (left) raised him, feeding him with a bottle. When Bailey was about a year and a half old and full grown, he was invited into the house. Sautner was surprised that Bailey didn't act like a bison in a china shop. One time, though, Bailey *did* have to back out of a room because he was too big to turn around. After a little exploring in the beginning, Bailey now mostly hangs out in the house watching TV, playing with kids, and joining holiday dinners. "I raised six kids before Bailey," Sautner says. "A bison is easy."

Weighing about as much as you and 27 of your friends, the bison is the largest land mammal in North America.

Both male and female bison have beards.

FIRE-FIGHTING FISH

EAGAN, MINNESOTA, U.S.A.

Turns out the water in Dory the betta fish's glass home was handy for more than just breathing. He "used" it to put out a fire at the school where he lives! When someone accidentally left a candle burning after school, the box beneath the candle caught fire. Flames spread to papers and books near Dory, and eventually the heat shattered the glass. Water gushed over the flames, putting them out. Firefighters met only smoke—and an unhappy-looking Dory flopping in two inches of water. Now in a new tank in a new classroom, Dory is the class favorite. Looks like a fish rules in this school!

Bettas can breathe the oxygen from both air and water, thanks to a special organ above their gills.

PELICAN SWALLOWS DOG!

HÖRSTEL, GERMANY

Don't try to take a treat from *this* pelican! At least that's the lesson Katijina the Australian ridgeback dog learned when she stole a frozen chicken treat from Petri the pelican one afternoon. The result? Petri poked around the dog's mouth, prodded inside her ear, and then even tried to swallow Katijina's head—all in search of the missing snack. "Little did Petri know that Katijina ate the treat in one bite," says Roland Adams, who owns the sanctuary where Katijina and Petri live with other dogs, birds, rabbits, and monkeys. Adams says the animals get along peacefully—most of the time. "It helps that Katijina just had puppies," he says. "It made her much more patient with Petri."

Petri can't find her treat in Katijina's ear, either!

A pelican uses its extendable throat under its beak as a net to catch fish.

Petri the pelican playfully tries to make a treat out of Katijina's head.

COW SCARES BEAR

LONGMONT, COLORADO, U.S.A.

Laid-back cows are usually no match for ferocious bears. Try telling that to Apple the cow, who chased a young black bear away after he stumbled into her pasture. "The bear jumped on top of a fence and got close enough to Apple that they were actually touching noses," says Penny Cox, who lives nearby and witnessed the action. After an intense stare-down between the curious animals, the bear fell off the fence and into the field. Then Apple chased him into the nearby woods. "She was bellowing and mooing the whole way," Cox says. Some people assumed that Apple was fiercely protecting her property, but owner Nancy Dayton thinks her cow was being friendly. "It's easy to paint Apple as this threatening 'watch cow,'" she says. "But I think she saw the bear as a buddy and was just trying to play."

YIKES! THAT'S THE WEIRDEST-LOOKING BEAR I'VE EVER SEEN!

A bear's strong claws help it climb even the tallest trees.

DOG EATS FROM HIGH CHAIR

GRAND RAPIDS, MICHIGAN, U.S.A.

Tink, a silver Labrador retriever, has a rare digestive disorder that makes it difficult for food to move from her mouth all the way down to her stomach. This means that Tink has to eat sitting upright, so that gravity can do its thing and help get those delicious morsels into her belly. Luckily for Tink, her owner, Tom Sullivan, would stop at nothing to get the precious pup what she needs. Tom turned to the internet for help, and soon a crowd of dog-loving Good Samaritans had donated the funds for a special doggy high chair. But it doesn't stop there—Tink also has to be burped like a human baby! After every meal, she is picked up and gently massaged to ensure that all of her food digests properly. When she's not chowing down in her chair, Tink has a completely normal doggy life and often hams it up for her fans online. Better yet, she is helping raise awareness for other dogs with special needs, and proving that pups with unique conditions can lead full and healthy lives.

A dog high chair is also called a Bailey Chair.

WHAT AM I SUPPOSED TO DO? MY FRIDGE IS FULL.

CHIPMUNK GOES NUTS

DEMOTTE, INDIANA, U.S.A.

When Hope Wideup spotted a chipmunk scurrying off with her gardening glove, she later found it under her car's hood. So when her car wouldn't start a few weeks later, she figured the chipmunk was to blame. Only this time it wasn't a glove. The chipmunk had hidden his winter hoard of black walnuts—hundreds of them—under the hood.

It's not so weird for a chipmunk to store lots of nuts and seeds in a single place. During the winter, they take frequent naps lasting several days, called *torpor states.* "And they're going to be looking for a snack when they wake up," says wildlife expert Judy Loven. But Loven thinks this chipmunk is unique. Almost all the cases of nuts hidden in cars involve sneaky tree squirrels. "Hopefully this chipmunk doesn't give his friends any ideas," she says.

A chipmunk can store about a teaspoon's worth of seeds or nuts in each cheek pouch.

PUPPIES SAVE LOST KID

VIRGILINA, VIRGINIA, U.S.A.

Jaylynn Thorpe's family was terrified when the three-year-old wandered off into the woods on a frigid 17°F night. Thankfully, the puppies, Bootsy and Dipstick, wandered off with him—and probably saved his life.

While rescue workers searched for Jaylynn with scent-sniffing dogs and a heat-seeking helicopter, the puppies nestled around the shivering boy. They pressed against him all night and kept him warm—and alive. Says veterinarian Emily Kinnaird, "They snuggled to keep warm."

Twenty hours later, rescuers were nearby. But a scared Jaylynn hid beneath a pile of leaves. Once again, the puppies played the heroes, barking to alert the rescue team. Jaylynn soon was reunited with his family, cold and hungry but unhurt. "The puppies were very important to his survival," says fire chief Chad Loftis.

Jaylynn with his pooch pals

They treated him like another puppy in their litter.

Bootsy (left) and Dipstick

TORTOISE LUVS 2 SK8

JERUSALEM, ISRAEL

No one expects tortoises to be speed demons. But when Arava the African spurred tortoise got a "skateboard" for her back legs, she became speedier than most.

Arava had arrived at the Jerusalem Biblical Zoo unable to move her hind legs. "She wouldn't eat and tucked her head inside her shell," says veterinarian Nili Avni-Magen. "She seemed so sad." The medical staff couldn't find a reason for the paralysis, but they had a solution: wheels!

Arava could still use her front legs, so a metalworker built a two-wheeled metal platform with straps to go around Arava's shell. When Arava first tried out her "skateboard," she took a few steps with her front legs and started rolling. Now she zips around her enclosure on her board, "outrunning" the other tortoises. Arava has a long life to look forward to—unless she tries to ollie out of a ramp.

HEY, WHERE ARE THE BRAKES ON THIS THING?

Tortoises like Arava can live to be 70 years old.

41

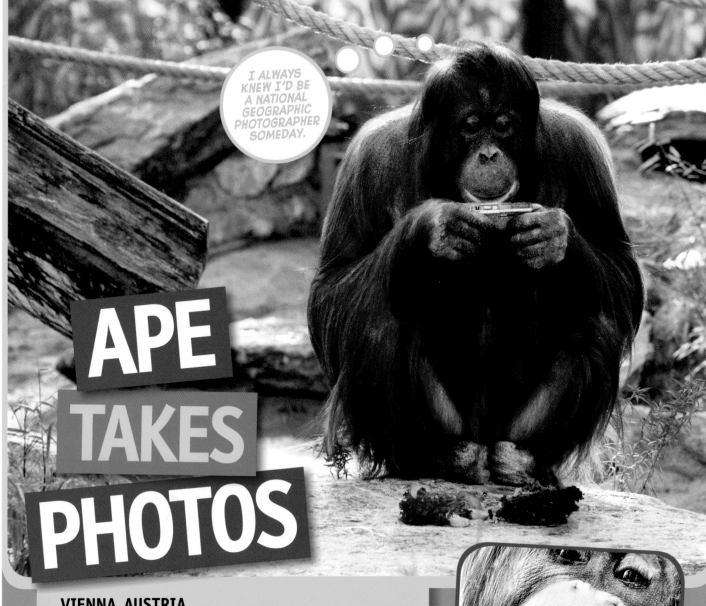

I ALWAYS KNEW I'D BE A NATIONAL GEOGRAPHIC PHOTOGRAPHER SOMEDAY.

APE TAKES PHOTOS

VIENNA, AUSTRIA

You probably take lots of pictures at the zoo. But at Schönbrunn Zoo, Nonja the orangutan might take pictures of *you*.

Nonja received a camera as a toy and was soon taking pictures of her world. The ape has action shots of her roommates swinging from their forest-like jungle gym and still lifes of their food. Nonja also shoots self-portraits, including a close-up of her licking the lens (right). Keepers have posted more than 150 photos online, making Nonja an Internet sensation.

Talented photographer? Maybe not. Keepers suspect she's more motivated by getting a treat than taking pictures: Every time Nonja clicks the camera, a raisin pops out. "Nonja isn't interested in her photos," says zoo deputy director Harald Schwammer. "But she likes raisins a lot."

Self-portrait

DOG RUNS HALF MARATHON

A bloodhound can follow a scent for more than 130 miles (209 km).

ELKMONT, ALABAMA, U.S.A.

In the town of Elkmont, Alabama, folks were delighted when a bloodhound named Ludivine joined in on a fund-raiser half marathon. Ludivine had been let out to do her business, but snuck out of her yard and made her way to the race-course—all without her owner knowing! She joined the rest of the racers, quickly charmed her competitors ... and raced past them. Even though she paused to splash in streams and sniff new scents, the hilarious hound ran the entire 13.1 miles (21 km) and managed to finish in seventh place. She even received a medal! And best of all, Ludivine's doggy dash caught the attention of several newspapers, bringing tons of attention to the fund-raiser. Ludivine's run was so inspiring that the organizers of the marathon even changed its name—it is now called the Hound Dog Half Marathon.

SEAL SNATCHES FISH

NOW ... WHAT'S FOR DESSERT?

This seal snacked on trout she stole from this hatchery.

SANDWICH, MASSACHUSETTS, U.S.A.

Employees at a trout hatchery walked into a crime scene. The crook? A young harbor seal. Her crime? Stealing fish straight from the hatchery's waters.

The seal broke in during the night and gulped down unknown numbers of whole trout before she was caught. To get to her booty, the sea-dwelling mammal slogged up a creek, across a marsh, and through shallow water tunnels that ran under a mini-golf course, a highway, and eventually the hatchery's fence. Total distance: two miles. "That's really far from the beach," says Katie Moore of the International Fund for Animal Welfare. "I've never seen anything like it."

Moore's crew gently netted the bandit and released her back into the ocean, where fish are a lot harder to catch. But the seal probably didn't need a meal right away. "She had a big ole belly full of fish!" Moore says.

7 ANIMALS SAVE THE DAY

Would an animal care enough to save another creature's life? Some experts say absolutely not. But these heartwarming stories of animal heroism seem to tell a different tale.

I'M NOT AFRAID OF BULL-IES!

1

DOGS CHASE BULLS AWAY!

SAND CREEK, WISCONSIN, U.S.A.

An angry bull violently tossed farmer Roger Hanson into the air and then rammed him from the back. The animal then tossed him again as another bull bellowed, waiting his turn. Hanson's wife unleashed their 135-pound Great Dane. But the silly dog just wanted to play. Hanson had locked their miniature rat terriers—Jack, Jill, and Mary—inside a truck because they had been teasing the bulls earlier. Now they were yelping at the sight of their owner being attacked. "Get the little dogs!" Hanson gasped. Mrs. Hanson opened the truck door. "They roared out like a team of horses," she says. The three flew at the nearly 2,000-pound rampaging bulls and nipped at their ankles. Courageously, the little dogs stood their ground under the stomping hooves, then chased the bulls into the pasture. But the dogs' good deeds weren't quite over. Mr. Hanson had broken his leg and many ribs in the attack. Who came to the hospital to cheer him up? Jack, Jill, and Mary!

2

DOG RESCUES
KANGAROO

IT SOUNDS CRAZY, BUT I SAW THIS THING CALLED A HUMAN THAT WALKS ON TWO LEGS!

TORQUAY, AUSTRALIA

Rex the pointer dog mix had returned from his walk when he started acting excited, pointing at a dead kangaroo that had been hit by a car the night before. "I was worried he had found a snake, so I called him back," says Rex's owner, Leonie Allan. But the dog didn't listen. Instead, Rex picked up something in his mouth and gently dropped it at Allan's feet. It was a baby kangaroo that had survived in its mother's pouch! "Rex did not leave that joey's side until I figured out what to do," Allan says. Soon she took the 'roo—nicknamed Rex Junior—to Jirrahlinga Koala & Wildlife Sanctuary. A few weeks later on a visit, Rex instantly recognized his friend and playfully nudged and licked the delighted kangaroo. The dog was following his retrieving instincts when he saved the joey, but maybe he was following his heart, too.

3

CAT DETECTS DEADLY GAS

BEATS SNIFFING MY LITTER BOX.

NEW CASTLE, INDIANA, U.S.A.

As the Keesling family slept, a silent killer was filling their home. A hole in a fuel line was pumping life-threatening amounts of carbon monoxide—a deadly, odorless gas—into the house. Fourteen-year-old Michael was overcome by fumes and passed out in the hall. That's when Winnie the cat sniffed something amiss and wouldn't stop till she awakened her owners. "Winnie was meowing into my ear like a siren," Cathy Keesling says. "She kept running up and down all over the bed and pulling my hair to wake me up." Keesling could barely find the strength to call 911. Good thing she did. If help had arrived just five minutes later, it would have been too late. For her bravery, Winnie received the ASPCA's Cat of the Year award—and superhero status among her family.

A domestic cat can sprint about 31 miles an hour.

NORTH EAST, MARYLAND, U.S.A.

Debbie Parkhurst panicked when she started choking on a piece of apple. "I couldn't breathe," she says. "I began beating my chest to save myself." But Toby the golden retriever seemed to know something was wrong. As if by instinct, Toby sprang into action, leaping up onto Parkhurst with both paws, pushing her to the ground, and bouncing furiously on her chest—an action similar to the Heimlich maneuver, which forces blocked items from the windpipe. The apple dislodged and Parkhurst, gasping for air, threw her arms around her loyal rescuer. Doctors say Toby's actions saved his owner's life, which surprised her a bit. "He was always the class clown, not the hero type," Parkhurst says. "He even ate his training school diploma."

4 POOCH RESCUES CHOKING OWNER

5

NEXT TIME I'LL SAY, "STOP, IN THE NAME OF THE LAW!"

BIRD ALARMS
BURGLARS

LEOMINSTER, MASSACHUSETTS, U.S.A.
The pet shop had been robbed twice before. But the third time, Merlin—a large blue-and-gold macaw—was waiting. Early one morning, thieves shattered the store's window and crept inside, only to be startled by a mighty voice shouting from the back room. Fearing they weren't alone, the robbers took off with only a handful of change. "When Merlin talks, it's loud and clear," says Victor Montalvo, a friend of the store owner. Police believe that Merlin began yelling, "Rhonda! Rhonda!" (the name of his former owner) and frightened the crooks away. They haven't returned since. Merlin might say that he's "a pretty bird," but he's a pretty smart bird, too.

A macaw's first and fourth toes point backward to help it climb and hold food.

6 RABBIT SAVES COUPLE
FROM FIRE

Rabbit is a bunny like the one pictured here.

MELBOURNE, AUSTRALIA
When a faulty heater started a fire in the home of Michelle Finn and Gerry Keogh early one morning, the couple remained asleep. But their long-eared rabbit, named Rabbit, was wide awake—and began pounding furiously at his enclosure. "Rabbit was making all sorts of sounds and noises," Finn says. "He was frantically thumping and jumping at the walls of his cage." Finn and Keogh woke to find their house engulfed in flames and narrowly escaped with Rabbit. The home was destroyed, but Finn found at least one hopeful outcome: "It makes you appreciate the unconditional love you receive from your pet."

HERE I COME TO SAVE THE DAY!

7

DOG SAVES BOY FROM DROWNING

NORTH BEND, NEBRASKA, U.S.A.

Tony Bailey had gone swimming in the Platte River lots of times. But one day, not realizing that heavy rains had caused a raging river current, the 12-year-old jumped in and found himself in danger of being swept downstream. As the boy struggled to cling to an anchored tire with his foot, Tony shouted for help. But no one heard his calls. Becoming more and more exhausted, Tony thought he was a goner—until Jake the Labrador retriever leaped into the dangerous waters and swam to Tony's rescue. "He knew I wasn't playing around and really needed help," he says. The boy wrapped one arm around Jake's neck and the two swam to the bank, where Tony thanked his four-legged lifesaver with a soggy hug.

No wonder Labrador retrievers enjoy the water: Their coats are water-repellent and their paws have webbing between the toes.

POOCHES SURVIVE ON TWO LEGS!

PORT WASHINGTON, NEW YORK, U.S.A.
Carmen, Venus, and Pablo chase each other, play hide-and-seek, and steal the remote control off the coffee table. The Chihuahua triplets don't seem to notice they were born with only their two hind legs.

Venus shows she's a stand-up gal.

Staff and volunteers at North Shore Animal League America took months to teach the dogs the skills they'd need to thrive. The three exercised in a pool to build up their muscles and learned to use carts (below) that support them as if they have front legs. The pooches were even put in harnesses that made them look like marionettes. That helped them develop better balance so they could bend forward to drink from a water bowl.

"Today they can walk like people, hop like kangaroos, and move like dogs in their carts," says Donna Imhof, who adopted all three. Carmen, Venus, and Pablo have human help, but they also help each other. They hold bones for each other and clean each other's ears. Looks like these guys know the meaning of family support.

Chihuahuas were named after a state in Mexico.

Carmen, Venus, and Pablo use their carts as front legs.

DOES THIS MEAN THAT, YES, I AM SMARTER THAN A FIFTH GRADER?

CHIMP OUTSMARTS HUMANS

KYOTO, JAPAN

Think you're brainier than a chimpanzee? Most people do—unless they've met Ayumu the chimp. According to researchers, he has a better memory than most humans.

Ayumu and three other chimps took the same memory test as college students. Numbers in random order flashed on a screen, then turned into white squares. Participants had to touch the squares in numerical order to demonstrate memory skills. Ayumu was so accurate he outscored other chimps *and* students.

Scientist Tetsuro Matsuzawa, who led the study, says many people think humans are better than animals in every way. He says this test proves that isn't always true and hopes his research will motivate people to treat animals with more respect. "We need to recognize that we are all members of the animal kingdom," he says. That's good advice for chimps *and* humans.

I DON'T KNOW WHY HE'S SMILING. I JUST PULLED OFF HIS EAR.

OCTOPUS ♥S TOY

NEWQUAY, ENGLAND, U.K.

Louis the giant Pacific octopus has a favorite toy: Mr. Potato Head. He plays with it for hours, pulling at it with his eight arms. Even after he has disassembled the toy, he wants Mr. Potato Head all to himself. Aquarium workers who try to fish out the parts get playfully attacked by the octopus.

Louis may sound like an octopus in love, but that's not really the case. Aquarium workers hide food inside Mr. Potato Head, and Louis enjoys the hide-and-seek challenge. "It keeps him from getting bored," says Matt Slater, aquarium curator at Blue Reef Aquarium. Plus, the octopus may like the smooth shape and flexible arms. "Octopuses feed on crustaceans, and Mr. Potato Head must feel like a crab," Slater says. Good thing there's food inside. Otherwise Louis might try to eat the toy spud like a baked potato.

Louis's previous toys included LEGO bricks and a toy boat.

SHEEP THINKS HE'S A DOG

WHERE'S THE NEAREST FIRE HYDRANT?

COLCHESTER, ENGLAND, U.K.

Billy the sheep likes to hang out with his flock. But his flock isn't made up of sheep—it's a pack of dogs!

Billy was "adopted" by the dogs after he was orphaned at birth. "Two of my dogs spent hours licking him when I brought him home," says wildlife rescuer Rosie Catford. Today Billy is an official member of the pack. Every morning, the sheep waits by the gate until his friends come out of the house. They take walks together, chase each other, and even play ball. "Wherever the dogs are, that's where Billy is," Catford says.

How do you explain this "dog" in sheep's clothing? "Billy was brought up by dogs, so he thinks he's a dog," says livestock expert Temple Grandin. "He's going to try to act like a dog as much as he can." Catford agrees . . . sort of: "Whether Billy thinks he's a dog or whether he thinks the dogs are sheep is anyone's guess!"

SEAL PUP MYSTERY

CARFORTH, ENGLAND, U.K.

The last thing anyone expected to see in the middle of a country road was a seal pup. But there was Ghost, two miles from the nearest river and eight miles from his ocean habitat. How did the motherless youngster get so far from home?

"You never see seals this far inland," says wildlife rescuer Nick Green. "I figured whoever reported the seal had made a mistake." Seals often hunt where rivers meet the sea, so one possibility is that Ghost swam too far upriver and got lost. But the fact that he left the river and made the difficult journey over land stunned rescuers. "They feel safest in the water," Green says. "This was extremely unusual, and we'll never know the reason."

Luckily, Ghost was healthy and unharmed, so he was released back into the Irish Sea less than two weeks later. "He swam right off," Green says. The mystery remains unsolved, but at least the story has a happy ending.

> Seal pups can swim and dive when they're just a few hours old.

PIG SAVES OWNER

> Potbellied pigs are by nature protective of their herd, according to pig expert Marcie Christensen. Dasiey was so protective of her "herd" of humans that she'd sometimes head butt visitors in the Joneses' house!

LAS VEGAS, NEVADA, U.S.A.

Jordan Jones was playing outside when out of nowhere a growling pit bull angrily lunged toward him. Terrified, the boy could barely react. But just in the nick of time, Jordan's potbellied pig Dasiey jumped in front of the pit bull, fending off the dog.

Jordan's mom, Kim Jones, heard Dasiey's squeals and ran outside. "Jordan was just frozen, not moving," she says. "Dasiey was backed into a corner but still standing up to the dog." At one point Dasiey's head was locked in the pit bull's jaws. But she refused to give up.

Jordan's dad finally untangled Dasiey and the pit bull. Jordan was fine, as was Dasiey after a few stitches. "If Dasiey hadn't been there, the pit bull would've attacked Jordan," Jones says. "Dasiey will always be our hero."

OUR ^^ IS A SNATCHER Please take these if yours!!

Willy guards his stash of gloves.

CAT STEALS GLOVES

PELHAM, NEW YORK, U.S.A.

Willy the cat is a great hunter. Problem is, Willy hunts gloves! Last year, Willy started stealing gardening gloves from the neighbors. Usually collecting pairs—retrieving them one at a time—he'd leave one on the front porch of owner Jennifer Pifer's house, and the other on her back porch.

Many cats will leave dead prey as "gifts" for their owners, but no one is sure why Willy chose to offer up gloves. "I don't even wear gloves when I garden," Pifer says. "Maybe Willy thinks I should." Without a clue about how to find the owners, Pifer strung up the gloves on her fence with a friendly note asking neighbors to take theirs. People might want to keep an eye on their shoes, too!

BIRD *NABS* BURGLAR!

WILLIAMSPORT, PENNSYLVANIA, U.S.A.

Who needs a guard dog when you have Sunshine the macaw? He helped catch a thief!

Sunshine's owner, J.W. Erb, had returned home to a ransacked apartment. "I wasn't worried about my stuff," Erb says. "But when I saw feathers everywhere, total fear set in." Luckily Erb found an unharmed Sunshine hiding in the bedroom. "The thief probably thought he'd steal Sunshine, too, but I know my bird," Erb says. "He wasn't going for it, and I knew the guy lost the fight."

Erb told police to be on the lookout for someone who looked as if he had been attacked by a wild animal. "After the police arrested the suspect, they told me he looked as if he'd been in a fight with barbed wire," Erb says. That's all police needed to connect the thief with Sunshine—and the break-in. Seems this macaw turned a cat burglar into a jailbird.

Sunshine (shown below with owner J.W. Erb) likes to dance in the shower.

Both male and female macaws are very colorful. That's rare in the bird world. Usually the male is more brightly colored.

I HOPE HE DOESN'T THINK I'M A FLY.

FROG GIVES MOUSE A LIFT

LUCKNOW, INDIA

What's a mouse to do when it's floating up a street without a paddle? Hitch a ride on a frog!

Swept up in a flooded street during a monsoon—a heavy rainfall that can cause flooding—the mouse might have been a goner had this frog not swum by. "Frogs are at home in the water, so they easily weather these storms," says biology professor Jim Ryan. "Mice aren't strong swimmers. They'll use anything as a life preserver or raft."

Is the frog a hero? It's doubtful. "The mouse probably grabbed onto the first thing that went by," Ryan says. "It was probably just a very tolerant frog—and a very lucky mouse!"

Frogs were the first land animals with vocal cords.

55

THIS SURE BEATS LIVING IN A TREE.

SQUIRREL RAISED BY DOG!

Finnegan the squirrel often snuggled (top) and fed (above) alongside Maddy's pups.

SEATTLE, WASHINGTON, U.S.A.

Finnegan the squirrel had an unlikely mother—a dog named Maddy. Local wildlife rescuer Debby Cantlon had taken in the orphaned three-day-old squirrel. But Maddy had her own ideas about who would raise Finnegan.

Maddy was about to give birth and decided she had enough love for one more. The seven-pound pooch dragged the caged squirrel through two rooms, down a hallway, past a bathroom, into the bedroom, and next to her dog bed. "I tried moving Finnegan away, but Maddy just pulled him back," Cantlon says. After Maddy gave birth, she licked Finnegan as if he were a newborn, nursed him, and allowed him to sleep among her pups.

Finnegan soon went back to the wild but returns to Cantlon's house for an occasional meal. He doesn't visit alone, though—he brings a female friend and their two babies!

OWL *RIDES* BIKE

ECCLESHALL, ENGLAND, U.K.

Treacle the owl has a strange hobby: He's a biking fanatic. Gentleshaw Wildlife Centre owner Jenny Morgan wondered if the lazy Treacle, who has lived at the center since he was a chick, would like riding on her bike. She set him on the handlebars, where he happily perched while she pedaled. Now she and her feathered friend ride together a couple of times a week. He usually just watches the scenery go by—except when the ride gets bumpy. Then he turns his head to stare at her! Could cycling become a favorite activity of the other captive birds? Not likely. "The birds give Treacle a rather odd look," Morgan says. "It's not exactly a normal hobby for an owl."

ANYONE KNOW WHERE I CAN GET AN OWL-SIZE HELMET?

Treacle's owner doesn't allow him to ride all the time. He needs to fly to exercise his wings.

ALIEN *INVADES* AQUARIUM?

SOUTHSEA, ENGLAND, U.K.

This creature has a secret. It's not that she's an alien from another planet. The secret is that although the creature—a baby thornback ray—appears to have a happy face, she doesn't have a face at all! What you see here is actually two nostrils and a mouth on the ray's underside. Nicknamed "Little Ray of Sunshine" by keepers at Blue Reef Aquarium, the ray spends most of her time hiding under sand. So like other rays, her eyes are on the top side of her body to watch for prey. In this picture, Sunshine had spotted a worker who feeds her and had swum up against the side of the tank to grab some grub. Sunshine may not really be smiling, but she sure seems glad that it's dinnertime.

NINE LIVES

CEDAR, MINNESOTA, U.S.A.

Hope the cougar loves tossing a basketball in the air with her front paws. But not long ago her survival wasn't a slam dunk. Found in a cage on an Iowa farm, the abused animal was starving and had frostbitten ears. Workers at the Wildcat Sanctuary, where the animal was taken, named her "Hope." But the vet didn't think the cougar would survive.

Hope's starved body couldn't digest much food. So every few hours, workers hand-fed Hope raw chicken with powdered vitamins sprinkled on top. Soon the cougar began gaining weight—and showing signs she was a survivor. "We gave her the tools, but she did it on her own," says Tammy Quist of the sanctuary. "Hope chose to live."

The cougar has gained 43 pounds and lots of spunk since her rescue. Besides playing with her basketballs, Hope likes to give other cougars a playful thump on the head. "Everything is fun for her," Quist says. "She's just like a kitten!"

Hope recovered, but when she was found, she weighed 40 pounds less than a typical adult female cougar.

A cougar is also called a puma or a mountain lion.

TORTOISE LOVES TOY

I HEAR TEENAGE MUTANT NINJA TURTLES IS PLAYING AT THE MOVIES. WANNA GO?

CORNWALL, ENGLAND, U.K.

Timmy the tortoise won't go to sleep until his best friend, Tanya, is right there with him. Nothing strange about that—except that Tanya is a plastic tortoise. "They spend their days together," says Joy Bloor, who runs the Tortoise Garden. "If Timmy wants to go somewhere, he pushes Tanya along with him."

Timmy and Tanya have been "friends" for 20 years and came to the tortoise sanctuary when their owner moved. At first Bloor put Timmy with real tortoises. "But they bit him and chased him away," she says. "Now he lives only with Tanya."

No one is sure if Timmy knows—or cares—that Tanya is plastic, or why he seeks out friendship in the first place. "Reptiles generally don't show affection like Timmy does," says tortoise expert Peter Pritchard. "It doesn't mean it's not possible." That's for sure: Timmy even tries to share his food with Tanya, nudging his lettuce toward her. Guess he wants her to eat her vegetables.

LAMB POST

Jacob is bold, but most sheep are timid. Flocks have been known to panic at a piece of paper blowing in the wind.

THAT'S THE WEIRDEST-LOOKING SHEEPDOG I'VE EVER SEEN.

CHESHIRE, ENGLAND, U.K.

Jacob the lamb is a bit confused—he thinks he's a sheepdog! When the fleecy baby was abandoned by his mother, Kip the sheepdog became the lamb's unofficial mom at Tatton Park's Home Farm. Soon Jacob started herding other animals—just like a sheepdog!

Jacob would run side by side with Kip as the dog did her work. If Kip rounded up sheep and ducks, so would Jacob. If Kip barked to keep the animals in line, Jacob would bleat. "He was Kip's shadow," says farm worker Jayne Chapman. "He did everything she did."

Jacob is now growing from lamb to ram. Although he has moved to a pasture with other sheep, he still isn't very sheepish. To Kip's dismay, Jacob still thinks he's a dog—and refuses to be herded!

ORANGUTAN SAVES HER BABY

SABAH, MALAYSIA

Emergency! A flooded river had trapped a wild orangutan mom and baby up a tree. The apes were gathering food in a tree on the bank of the Segama River when a flash flood hit, stranding them as the raging river overflowed.

Conservation groups rushed to the scene. Knowing it would be dangerous to interact directly with the protective mother, rescuers tossed her a rope they had tied to another tree. Amazingly, the orangutan knew what to do! With her baby clinging to her, the mother grasped the rope in one hand, dog-paddled to shore with the other, and disappeared into the rain forest. "We rarely see orangutans in the water," says primate expert Serge Wich of the Great Ape Trust in Iowa. "But these moms go to great lengths to save their babies."

With her baby holding on, the mother orangutan catches a rope.

Mom weighs her options.

Orangutans sometimes use their arms to swing through trees.

Slowly, the apes enter the water, and Mom swims to safety.

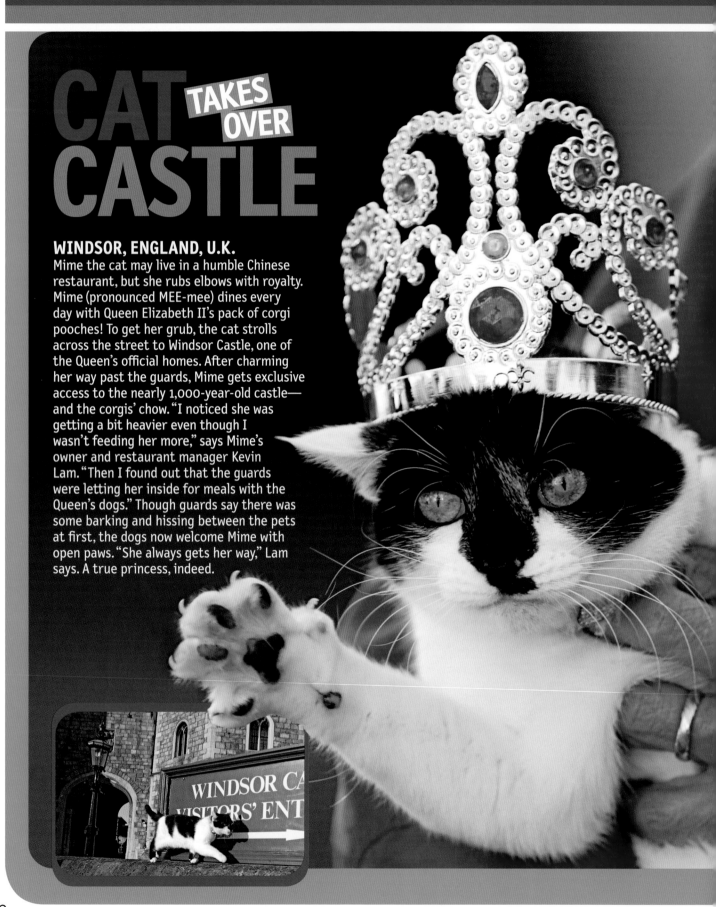

CAT TAKES OVER CASTLE

WINDSOR, ENGLAND, U.K.

Mime the cat may live in a humble Chinese restaurant, but she rubs elbows with royalty. Mime (pronounced MEE-mee) dines every day with Queen Elizabeth II's pack of corgi pooches! To get her grub, the cat strolls across the street to Windsor Castle, one of the Queen's official homes. After charming her way past the guards, Mime gets exclusive access to the nearly 1,000-year-old castle—and the corgis' chow. "I noticed she was getting a bit heavier even though I wasn't feeding her more," says Mime's owner and restaurant manager Kevin Lam. "Then I found out that the guards were letting her inside for meals with the Queen's dogs." Though guards say there was some barking and hissing between the pets at first, the dogs now welcome Mime with open paws. "She always gets her way," Lam says. A true princess, indeed.

WINDSOR CA
VISITORS' ENT

BOAR WELCOMES TOURISTS

I AM SO MUCH CUTER THAN THOSE DOLPHINS.

SHIP CHANNEL CAY, BAHAMAS

Forget the tropical fish and turquoise waters. Visitors to this tiny island in the Atlantic Ocean are more excited to spot Stones, a wild boar who has become a tourist attraction. Most wild boars spend their days sleeping in tall grass hiding from humans. But Stones runs on the beach, splashes in the ocean, and hams it up for cameras. "When visitors take pictures of Stones, he'll sit very still and stare straight ahead," says islander Mona Wiethüchter, who says Stones has been hanging around for years, ever since his mom brought him onto the beach to look for leftover human food. "When he's sleepy, he'll dig himself a hole in the sand, right between sunbathers." About 12 other wild boars live on the island, but Stones prefers to be around his people pals. "He isn't interested in having other animal friends," Wiethüchter says. "He likes to hang out wherever we are as the center of all the action."

BEAR GOES FOR DRIVE

MAYBE I WOULD'VE GOTTEN FARTHER ON A BIKE.

HIGHLAND LAKES, NEW JERSEY, U.S.A.

This bear didn't steal just food—he made off with a car! Sharon Terzakis woke up one morning to find her SUV mysteriously down the hill in a neighbor's yard. A patrolling police officer quickly determined that the "theft" was no professional job: Sticky drool, coarse black hair, and claw marks covered the car's interior, and a pile of candy wrappers dotted the floor. Turns out the culprit was a bear with a sweet tooth! All black bears have an excellent sense of smell and will do just about anything to get their paws on human food. This one sniffed out some leftover candy and broke in through the front window. "We think he released the car's emergency break, causing it to roll away," Terzakis says. Police jokingly posted "Wanted" signs around town, but it looks like the bear made a clean getaway.

BEAR DAMAGE!

PET HIPPO!

A typical meal for Jessica the hippo is sweet potatoes and dog food washed down with coffee.

"Time to watch American Idol!"

"Anyone for a piggyback ride?"

A hippo can fold its ears and nostrils shut to keep out water when it's swimming.

HOEDSPRUIT, SOUTH AFRICA

As a baby, Jessica slept in the same bed as humans Tony and Shirley Joubert. Now that she's bigger, she has to sleep with the dogs. But don't feel too bad for Jessica. After all, she *is* a hippo. And at almost 1,800 pounds, she would definitely break the bed!

The Jouberts adopted Jessica when the newborn hippo washed up in their riverfront yard. Tony, a former park ranger, got the go-ahead from the local authorities to raise the orphaned hippo as a pet. "We spoiled her rotten," Tony says. "Today she's just part of the family."

Jessica loves to go swimming with Shirley and give rides to kids. Wild hippos sometimes visit in the evening, but Jessica prefers to watch TV. And though the Jouberts think Jessica has gotten too big to come inside very often, it's hard to keep her out—she figured out how to open the front door with her lips.

GOLDFISH SURVIVES CHIMNEY DROP

MANSFIELD, ENGLAND, U.K.

Wanda is one lucky goldfish. The ten-inch-long fish cheated death twice. First, a hungry heron is thought to have plucked Wanda from a pond. Luckily, the bird dropped the goldfish—but not back into the water. The bird dropped Wanda down a chimney! After bouncing off a blazing fire, the fish landed on the hearth, flapping in a pile of soot. Resident Bill Brooks put the injured goldfish into some water and called animal rescuer Terry Marsh. "Wanda was in bad shape," says Marsh, who arrived to find the fish floating on its side with heron beak marks on its body. Marsh patiently nursed Wanda back to health. Now the feisty fish is back in a pond—this one deep enough to hide from hungry herons.

Goldfish were first domesticated by the Chinese.

1 Wanda's hero, Bill Brooks, stands outside his house.

2 Luckily no one was in the mood for roast fish the day that Wanda came.

3 Looks like nothing can stop this fish called Wanda.

PUPPY BATTLES BIG SNAKES

HOMESTEAD, FLORIDA, U.S.A.

Beagle versus giant python. It sounds like an unfair fight, but Python Pete the beagle has been trained to sniff out the Burmese pythons that threaten to overrun Florida's Everglades National Park.

The snakes, which can grow 20 feet long, have been illegally released by pet owners who didn't realize how large their baby snakes would become. The giant pythons are now breeding in the national park and preying on native animals.

Python Pete tracks down the giant snakes so they can be captured and removed by humans. To teach him tracking skills, trainer Lori Oberhofer puts snakes in burlap sacks and drags them around to lay down a scent. She's trained the dog to bark at the snakes from a safe distance, which is a good idea. No one wants this python tracker to become a snake snack!

Python Pete is part of the "Don't Let It Loose" campaign, which urges pet owners never to release unwanted pets into the wild.

DON'T LET IT LOOSE!
BE A RESPONSIBLE PET OWNER

BEAVERS BUSTED!

ST. HELENA PARISH, LOUISIANA, U.S.A.

Need cash? Some Louisiana beavers might be able to float you a loan! When police learned that bags of stolen money totaling $67,000 had been stashed in a creek, officers went to investigate. They began tearing down a beaver dam to lower the water level—and discovered hundreds of dollars in loose bills woven in with the dam's tree branches. "The bills were still whole," Major Michael Martin says. "They were just really muddy."

Beavers build dams from wood, but the resourceful rodents will add stones, plants, and even clothing. Apparently the beavers had found one of the money bags at the bottom of the creek, opened it, and used the bills like leaves!

Officers worked until midnight to gather up the loot and then dried the soggy bills in a clothes dryer. The thieves were caught. The beavers? They repaired the dam by morning. Maybe they should've kept enough cash to hire a carpenter!

Beavers wove the money they found into their dam (above).

66

"ROO'D" AWAKENING

DODGEVILLE, WISCONSIN, U.S.A.

You expect to see a cow in Wisconsin farm country, not a kangaroo. No wonder Sheriff Steve Michek thought the first call reporting the stray Australian animal was a prank. But sure enough, hopping around a woman's snowy yard was a five-foot-tall kangaroo!

So how *do* you catch a kangaroo? Michek lined up gates and cars to create a wide path leading into a horse barn. "We used apple slices to help him along," he says. Soon the 'roo bounded into the shelter, where he stayed until zoo officials arrived.

How the animal, now called Roo, got to Wisconsin remains a mystery. "He may have escaped in transit from somewhere," says Jim Hubing of the Henry Vilas Zoo, which adopted the animal. These days Roo is living a life of luxury as the zoo's newest star. Sure beats hopping around in the snow!

Kangaroos lick their forearms to stay cool.

SHARK TALE

WHAT'S FOR DINNER?

MONTEREY, CALIFORNIA, U.S.A.

Scuba divers cleaning this million-gallon tank wear a little something extra: chain mail. Why? Swimming close by—but not too close—is a great white shark nearly six-and-a-half feet long.

The shark made waves when she remained in captivity at the Monterey Bay Aquarium for 198 days, the longest ever for a great white. She came to her new home after fishermen accidentally caught her. Scientists at the aquarium used her visit to show that sharks should be protected, not feared. "Many species of sharks are threatened or endangered," says marine biologist Randy Kochevar.

Eventually, the shark was released into the ocean. Now she's back to catching her own dinner instead of grabbing it in the wild!

Great white sharks can have 3,000 teeth at any one time. But they're far more likely to munch on sea lions and fish than on you!

GORILLA WALKS LIKE A DUDE!

KENT, ENGLAND, U.K.

Apes rarely are mistaken for humans, but when Ambam the western lowland gorilla stands upright and starts strolling around on his feet, that's exactly what happens. "Some visitors think he's a man in a gorilla suit," says Phil Ridges, head gorilla keeper at Port Lympne Wild Animal Park, where Ambam lives.

Gorillas occasionally *do* walk on their hind legs, but they prefer to get around on all fours, their padded knuckles turning their hands into an extra pair of feet. But Ambam often walks upright, his arms swinging by his sides. "Ambam is more flexible than other gorillas, making it easier for him to stand," Ridges says. "And we think he likes walking on two feet so he can see over the walls and watch for his keepers bringing food."

People come from all over to see Ambam's humanlike moves. But the gorilla is taking the attention in stride. "For Ambam, walking this way is perfectly normal," Ridges says. "He has no idea what the fuss is all about."

DUCK FINDS WAY BACK HOME!

NORTH DEVON, ENGLAND, U.K.

Jake the Muscovy duck proved that love conquers all. He waddled for weeks to return to his sweetheart, Jemima!

Owner Roy Shindler had decided to give Jake to a friend eight miles away. When the duck vanished, the friend feared a hungry fox was responsible. But more than a month later, Jake shocked everyone and reappeared at his old home.

To return to Jemima, Jake weathered three snowstorms and risked animal attacks. And because the chubby duck couldn't fly more than a few feet off the ground, he had to find openings through four-foot-tall hedges blocking his path. "But the most remarkable part is the woods he had to cross," Shindler says. "Webbed feet aren't made for walking over such rough terrain."

On his return, Jake immediately cuddled up to Jemima. Says Shindler: "When he came back, they were like an old married couple."

1 "Maybe I should have taken a right turn back there."

2 "Tell me how much you missed me!"

Wild Muscovy ducks often hang out in trees.

CROSS-EYED OPOSSUM

LEIPZIG, GERMANY

At the Leipzig zoo, Heidi is just like any other opossum, except for one thing: her totally adorable and unique look. Unlike the other opossums, Heidi has crossed eyes. "Heidi is just like any opossum at our zoo," says the zoo's spokesperson Maria Saegebarth. Heidi hangs out with her sister and other opossum pals, and always pokes a curious head out of her house to say hello when her caretakers come around. Turns out Heidi doesn't even need good eyesight to survive—opossums rely on their sense of smell to find food and avoid predators in the wild. So Heidi might not know she's unique, but she still inspires countless visitors, spreading the message that unique equals awesome.

DOG BECOMES MAYOR

Brynn is not the only animal to become mayor—a cat, a cow, a goat, and other dogs have all been voted into office across the U.S.

RABBIT HASH, KENTUCKY, U.S.A.

In the town of Rabbit Hash, Kentucky, dogs rule and humans drool. At least, it's easy to get that idea once you meet the mayor—a five-year-old dog named Brynneth Pawltro! Brynneth, a pit bull, became the town's honorary mayor in 2017. Brynneth—or Brynn for short—was elected as part of a traditional fund-raiser in which residents of the small town donate a dollar to vote for their next mayor. This particular election managed to raise over $8,000, largely thanks to Brynn—she won in a landslide victory, beating contestants that included a cat and a donkey. According to the residents of Rabbit Hash, Brynn takes her job very seriously. Locals say that she greets visitors and loves children, and according to her owner, Brynn pledges not to chase cats. Luckily for this hardworking hound, being mayor isn't all business. The political pup loves to attend local festivals and soak up the sun—and, of course, get lots of treats and pets!

WORKIN' LIKE A DOG

VANCOUVER, BRITISH COLUMBIA, CANADA

Guests at the Fairmont Hotel Vancouver don't get greeted only by a doorman. They're also met by Mavis the Labrador retriever! When her first job as a Seeing Eye dog didn't work out, Mavis began "working" with her owner, a hotel manager. Paid in hot dogs, apples, and belly rubs, Mavis is "hired" to do jobs such as going for walks and playing in the park with hotel guests. When she's not working, Mavis chews her stuffed dog (which looks exactly like her) and checks her email ... sort of. "Guests like to send photos of their playtime with Mavis," says Lynn Gervais, who works at the hotel. "So she has her own personal email address." Next thing you know, Mavis may be instant messaging her customers!

WELCOME HOME

PARKERSBURG, WEST VIRGINIA, U.S.A.

Fred the monk parakeet is one smart bird. He escaped from his owners, survived four years in the wild, and then found his way back home!

Even though sightings of the bright green parakeet had been reported over the years, the Edwards family was shocked when he suddenly showed up in a friend's yard. "We knew it was him because he had the same chipped beak," says 12-year-old Aaron Edwards. The bird also kept repeating "What Fred," a nonsense saying he squawked before he escaped. Plus he snuggled up to his pals just like he used to. "It was as if he never left," Aaron's dad says.

Some things *had* changed, though. Fred stopped biting, and he now eats only birdseed instead of his previous favorite food, french fries. "I think he's relieved to be back," Aaron says. "It's like he thought, 'It's been a nice vacation, but it's time to go home.'"

A parakeet is a small parrot.

Monks are the only parrots that build nests out of sticks.

71

Willow also can "count." Owner Lyssa Howells holds different numbers of rocks, pennies, or treats in each hand, then asks the dog which is more or less. She always paws the correct answer.

DOG CAN READ

BANG

Scientists believe that dogs have the same mental capabilities as most 2- to 2½-year-old children.

SIT UP

NEW YORK, NEW YORK, U.S.A.

Willow the English terrier doesn't just hear commands from her owner—she also reads them. The pooch raises her paw when she sees the word "wave," lies down when she reads "bang," and gets on her hind legs at the sight of "sit up."

Lyssa Howells first used voice commands to teach Willow the tricks. Then she wrote each command on a flash card to hold up while she said the word at the same time. Soon the dog connected each written command with the right trick, without any vocal cues. "Willow is really intelligent," Howells says. "But I believe there's no such thing as an untrainable dog."

Animal behaviorist Bonnie Beaver thinks Willow doesn't read like you and I do. Instead, the dog probably recognizes the different shapes of each word. "Still, this is one special dog," she says. "Most people are lucky to have dogs that listen to you at all!"

Willow once had her own pet ferret named Walnut.

ARE WE THERE YET?

A swimming penguin's white belly blends in with sunlight above the ocean, "hiding" it from underwater predators.

SAN FRANCISCO, CALIFORNIA, U.S.A.

Talk about follow the leader! When six new Magellanic penguins arrived at the San Francisco Zoo, they immediately began swimming laps almost nonstop. Soon the other 46 penguins joined in, swimming from morning till night, only stopping to sleep and eat. "Sometimes it looked like a washing machine of tuxedos," says penguin keeper Jane Tollini. "There was nothing I could do to stop them!" Some even walked around the pool when it was drained for cleaning. Animal keepers figure the original six marathoners were mimicking the migration that wild Magellanic penguins do every year, up to 2,000 miles up the coasts of South America. Why the other 46 joined in the "migration" is still a mystery. Looks like these birds of a feather really *did* flock together!

Penguins can swim more than 20 miles an hour—four times speedier than the fastest human.

Magellanic penguins are the most common penguin species.

SCRATCH AND SNIFF

NEW YORK, NEW YORK, U.S.A.

Tillie the Jack Russell terrier gives new meaning to the term "Etch A Sketch." The canine artist scratches designs onto colored carbon paper taped on top of mat board. "She scopes out the board, using her tongue to kind of investigate where she wants to make her marks, then she goes into a frenzy," says owner-assistant Bowman Bastie. "I don't move her paws or anything." Tillie's career began when she started scratching on a notepad Bastie was writing on. Now Tillie has fans who buy the etchings, such as the one at right, for more than $100! Jokes Bastie: "I'm hoping she'll support *me* one day!"

MOVE OVER, PICASSO!

Last summer Tillie's art appeared in a museum exhibit.

LAW AND ORDER

Bert stands for "Be Enthusiastic, Responsible, and Truthful."

SAN DIMAS, CALIFORNIA, U.S.A.

Bert is the biggest sheriff's deputy in the West. He weighs 1,800 pounds and eats about 25 pounds of food a day. Not bad for a growing boy with three stomachs! Bert is a dromedary camel who was officially sworn in as a Los Angeles County deputy sheriff. He visits schools with his partner (and owner) Nance Fite to warn kids about the dangers of drugs. "People never forget Bert," Fite says. "So when kids think about Bert, hopefully they'll think about staying off drugs, too." Not many people would mess with Bert, but one animal can give the deputy a lickin'. When Fite tells her dog, Sally, to kiss the camel, Bert lies down and takes it in the face!

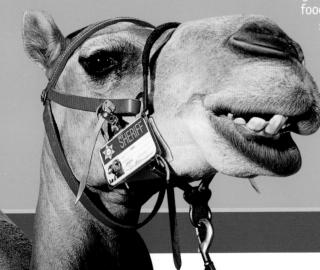

BONOBO "FLOSSES"!

WHAT DID I DO WITH MY ELECTRIC TOOTHBRUSH?

JACKSONVILLE, FLORIDA, U.S.A.

It's a picture sure to make any dentist smile: Lexi the bonobo "flossing" her teeth with string. But this ape's not really hooked on hygiene—she's just having fun. "Lexi is very curious, so when she pulled the string off of one of her toys, she put it in her mouth and played with it," says Tracy Fenn, who looks after Lexi at the Jacksonville Zoo and Gardens. "A photographer happened to be there at the right moment."

Close relatives of chimpanzees, bonobos are considered the smartest—and most playful—primates. Lexi is no exception. She'll spend her days doing somersaults and backflips around her habitat, which she shares with her family. Lexi is also the local babysitter. "She's always carrying the little ones around and helping the moms out," Fenn says. Too bad she can't teach them to brush their teeth.

There are more than 122 species of tree squirrels.

SQUIRRELVILLE

OLNEY, ILLINOIS, U.S.A.

Some towns honor their founders. This town honors albino squirrels! Olney is one of only three major albino squirrel colonies in the United States. Affected by a genetic defect, these pink-eyed critters have no color in their coats. And the rare furballs have the town by the tail. "Amy is really feisty," says Olney's unofficial squirrel nurse, Belinda Henton. "And Bubba likes to climb into people's pockets." Police wear a squirrel image on their badges and hand out fines to anyone bothering the squirrels. Cats must stay on leashes, and there are even squirrel crossing road signs. This is one place where it's a compliment to be called "squirrelly"!

In Thailand, a country in Southeast Asia, albino elephants are traditionally considered sacred.

THE GREAT ESCAPE

NEAR EMPANGENI, SOUTH AFRICA

Thula Thula Wildlife Reserve rangers, who were studying the reserve's six antelopes, observed the elephants nosing around. They assumed the animals were after some hay. Before they knew it, though, one elephant unfastened the gate's latches with her trunk and opened the gate!

The flabbergasted rangers watched as the antelopes bolted into the bush, followed by the elephants. It took the rangers hours to recapture the animals.

Why did the elephants do this? No one knows for sure. "But we know that elephants have a sense of humor," says elephant expert William Langbauer of the Pittsburgh Zoo & PPG Aquarium in Pennsylvania. "They may have just been having fun!"

An elephant's trunk has about 100,000 muscles and tendons.

With two fingerlike points on its trunk, an African elephant can pick up a 600-pound log or a marble-size fruit.

River otters have webbed feet and can swim underwater for a quarter of a mile before surfacing.

RIVER OTTER RESCUE

CLEARWATER, FLORIDA, U.S.A.

Charlie the river otter needed help. The six-week-old pup had been found wandering alone across a busy street. He was thin, dehydrated, and weighed less than three pounds. Trainers at the Clearwater Marine Aquarium were worried about the otter's health.

But Charlie was a fighter. Trainers began their rescue by feeding him with a bottle and taking him home every night. They snuggled him in towels and fed him vitamins.

Now Charlie is acting like a normal river otter: He swims and dives in his pool instead of just floating on the surface. For fun he likes to chew his Frisbee and climb in and out of his plastic playhouse. And when he's tired, Charlie crawls into his hammock and lounges tummy-up. "He's more like a real otter," says trainer Abbie Brewer. "But he still likes to suck his tail and toes like a baby!"

Charlie was named for a local student who raised more than $12,000 for aquarium programs.

MONKEY SEE, MONKEY DO

BOSTON, MASSACHUSETTS, U.S.A.

Ayla the capuchin monkey must be pretty smart: She goes to Monkey College! Along with 24 other monkeys, Ayla lives at a school that trains capuchins to assist disabled people who can't use their hands.

At the college, monkeys learn to help answer phones, change TV channels, load CDs, spoon-feed their human partners, and even scratch their itches. "They do everyday tasks that humans would use their hands for," says Judi Zazula, executive director of Helping Hands Monkey College. After one to two years of training, graduates are placed with disabled people, who direct the monkeys to their tasks with a mouth-operated laser pointer attached to the wheelchair.

Although many monkeys particularly enjoy jobs that involve pushing buttons, such as operating a computer, Ayla prefers turning book pages. She also likes to eat. Sometimes she opens the refrigerator, sneaks out a treat, and stashes it under a blanket for later!

Ayla operates a CD player (left) and a telephone (below).

Wild capuchin monkeys live in the treetops of the rain forests in Central and South America.

An Irish wolfhound's huge size makes some people nervous, but their kind and patient nature actually makes them bad watchdogs.

PARTY
ANIMAL

ABILENE, TEXAS, U.S.A.

Devlin the Irish wolfhound isn't a Republican or a Democrat, but this dog definitely has political connections! The pooch was elected to a second term as Dog Mayor of his city. More than 2,000 people voted for Devlin over Douglas the basset hound, Horatio the Chihuahua, and Sampson the Akita mix. Until he retired, the 165-pound wolfhound held office alongside the city's human mayor, "speaking" to audiences about animal rescue and adoption. Says owner Annette Turner: "When kids ask him questions, he barks out the answer and I translate."

7 AMAZING ANIMAL FRIENDS

Like humans, animals take care of each other. Sometimes it doesn't matter if they're different species. These stories prove that friendship comes in all shapes and sizes.

Sahara and Alexa

1

CATS AND DOGS LIVING TOGETHER

**CINCINNATI ZOO
AND BOTANICAL GARDEN, OHIO, U.S.A.**

Sahara, a cheetah cub, hissed as she faced Alexa the Anatolian shepherd puppy for the first time. The Anatolian is a Turkish dog bred to protect goats and sheep from predators such as cheetahs. It was important that Sahara and Alexa become friends. Elissa Knights, manager of the zoo's Cat Ambassador Program, wanted to use the two young animals in school presentations to teach U.S. students about the Cheetah Conservation Fund (CCF). In Namibia, in southern Africa, farmers don't want cheetahs around because they're concerned that the cats will kill their livestock. The CCF raises Anatolians and gives them to farmers to use as guard dogs. The cats just run away when the dogs bark.

Knights was wondering what would happen between Sahara and Alexa when suddenly her pet dog, Bailey, intervened. Snatching up a long, braided rope, Bailey stuffed the toy into Alexa's open mouth. Then he picked up the other end and took it to Sahara. She grabbed hold. The animals played tug-of-war, and a lasting friendship began. After that, Sahara and Alexa lived together at the zoo. Sahara regularly licks Alexa, who enjoys the affection. They sleep, play, and visit schools together. "They've worked out their differences," says Knights. "I know it's thanks to Bailey."

ORINDA, CALIFORNIA, U.S.A.

Nobody expected Simon the duck to lay an egg. Simon was supposed to be a "he," not a "she." But her owner, Jenny Maguire, got an even bigger surprise: Sitting atop Simon's egg trying to "hatch" it was Simon's best buddy, Snickers the rabbit!

Simon and Snickers met as classroom pets. Snickers spends his days herding his duck friend between Maguire's front yard and the back. If Snickers jumps out of sight, the duck quacks at the top of her lungs. "When Snickers hears her, he comes hopping!" Maguire says. At night they snuggle in a hay-filled bed. Once Simon had to go to the veterinarian's office for an overnight stay. But she missed her rabbit friend so much that she wouldn't stop quacking. She only stopped when Maguire finally brought Snickers to the clinic to spend the night. Simon must know that "somebunny" loves her!

2 QUACKY FRIENDSHIP

I KID YOU NOT: THIS GIRL IS MY BEST FRIEND.

DOG PROTECTS
GOAT
3

BUCKFASTLEIGH, ENGLAND, U.K.

When Lilly the goat arrived at Pennywell Farm after her mother abandoned her, humans weren't the only ones who cared for her. Billy the boxer did, too. Like an adoptive dad, Billy made sure Lilly kept her coat and muzzle clean by softly licking the milk the goat spilled on herself during bottle-feedings. Later, after the two playfully chased each other and it was time to go inside, Billy would gently nudge Lilly's bottom if she dawdled. When Billy leaped onto the sofa to watch TV, Lilly sprang up right next to him. "It's like Lilly has her own personal watchdog," owner Chris Murray says.

CAT PLAYS
WITH MARTEN
4

DOHR, GERMANY

After a mechanic discovered a marten—a weasel-like mammal—under a car's hood, the fuzzy fellow had no place to go. Luckily photographer Lothar Lenz adopted him—and so did Lenz's cat, Quarki. Quarki and the marten, named Bubub, are now inseparable and spend their days scampering up trees, climbing perches, and playing tag. That is, until the pals tire out. Then they curl up in a tiny box for a nap till they're ready to play some more. Says Lenz: "You hardly ever see one without the other."

5 ORANGUTAN KEEPS PET CAT

PANAMA CITY BEACH, FLORIDA, U.S.A.
Tonda the orangutan was sad when her mate went away. She even lost interest in painting, one of her favorite hobbies. Then her keepers introduced her to a cat named T.K.—and suddenly the ape was back to her old self. "Tonda carried T.K. all over the place," says Stephanie Willard of ZooWorld. "She gave him food, stroked him, and dangled toys for him to play with." The orangutan even covered T.K.'s eyes when the ape got her shots so the cat wouldn't be afraid. Tonda wouldn't come into her enclosure at night until T.K. was there, too. The cat even inspired Tonda to start painting again.

The word "orangutan" comes from two words in Asian languages: *orang*, meaning "man," and *utan*, meaning "of the forest."

SNOUT OUT 6

CAMBRIDGE, ONTARIO, CANADA
Great Danes were once bred to *hunt* wild pigs—not befriend them! And even though Fred the potbellied pig isn't exactly wild, the 40-pound porker and his 150-pound pooch pal, Earl, still make a very odd couple. "Earl is Fred's bodyguard," says their owner, Carol Lawrence. "If they come across an unfamiliar dog, Earl will put himself between the dog and Fred to make sure that Fred is in no danger." The two friends sleep in the same room, and when the pig goes outside, Earl follows to graze beside him on grass. But they only do *that* when they've finished eating their kibble-and-yogurt meal!

C'MON, FRED! SHOW THESE DOGS YOU'RE NO PORKER!

NIEDERSACSEN, GERMANY

After her mother was struck by a car, Finchen the fawn was brought to live on a farm. One day as she grazed, a wild rabbit appeared, and it's been by Finchen's side ever since. "I've watched them alert each other to hazards or predators so they can flee to safety," says Tanja Askani, who photographed the pair. But Finchen and her rabbit friend seem to be more than each other's protectors. The rabbit must have realized that Finchen was too big to sleep underground, because the bunny built a grassy nest that was big enough for them both to curl up in. They're like a real-life Bambi and Thumper.

7

RABBIT BUILDS BED FOR DEER

HEALING HOOVES

JUST CALL ME DOCTOR PETIE!

AKRON, OHIO, U.S.A.

Horsing around is allowed at Akron Children's Hospital—at least when Petie visits! Hospitals can be scary, so the Shetland pony–miniature horse mix brings fun and comfort to sick kids. "Some kids haven't smiled for a long time, but they light up when they see Petie," trainer Susan Miller says. "He lays his head on the children's beds, and his eyes get big and soft."

The pony gets three baths and is sprayed with safe-for-horses disinfectant before making his hospital rounds. (That's to make sure he's superclean for the patients.) After every visit Miller rewards Petie with his favorite treats: peppermint candy and popcorn. Then he goes back to his farm, where he likes to chase other horses and sneak out of his pen. Says Miller: "Petie is an angel at the hospital, but at home he's a little devil!"

Petie makes a patient smile.

CREATURE FROM THE BLACK LAGUNA

Old Bob is 30 to 50 years old. He could live to be 100.

FULLERTON, CALIFORNIA, U.S.A.

Was there a monster in Laguna Lake? For 30 years fishermen told tales of "Old Bob," a beast that gulped ducks and snapped fishing lines. Most figured he was just a legend. But during a lake cleanup, workers netted a prehistoric-looking turtle with scary jaws and long claws. "He freaked us out!" says Peter Path, who was in charge of the cleanup.

Old Bob is an alligator snapping turtle. The turtles are native to the southeastern United States, so he's probably a former pet. In the lake he grew into a 100-pound lump of attitude. "When I put a thick bamboo pole in his mouth, he snapped it like a toothpick," Path says. Old Bob doesn't have the skills to survive in his native environment with other snappers. That's why he soon headed to a new home, where he is likely still legendary: for grumpiness!

Alligator snapping turtles have pink, worm-shaped pieces of flesh on their tongues that they use like fishing lures. When a fish tries to grab the "worm," *CHOMP!*

SMART DOG

DORTMUND, GERMANY

Rico is an old dog teaching scientists new tricks. The border collie understands more than 250 words!

Experts think the average pet dog can understand about 20 commands. But Rico can fetch any of his 260 toys—from "dinosaur" to "Santa Claus" to "octopus"—as well as follow dozens of commands. But what really excites scientists is that Rico can learn new words without the repetitive training that most dogs need.

For instance, Rico's owner can place an unfamiliar baseball among seven familiar toys and then say, "Get me the baseball." Rico has never connected the word "baseball" with the new toy, but he retrieves it. Why? Rico knows the names of the seven other toys, so he understands that the baseball is the toy his owner wants.

Until Rico, many scientists thought only humans learned through the process of elimination. They are now looking for other dogs with Rico's intelligence. "We think more are out there, mostly border collies and Labrador retrievers," says Julia Fischer, a biologist who studied Rico. "Dogs like Rico are truly exceptional."

Rico fetches one of his 260 toys.

Participants are cautioned to wear formfitting clothes and to keep their hair up, as the goats like to chew anything and everything!

GOATS TAKE YOGA

MONROE, OREGON, U.S.A.

When the founder of Goat Yoga, Lainey Morse, welcomed goats onto her farm, she had no idea that it would be the start of something huge. Lainey already knew that the presence of goats could lower stress, and she was a huge fan of using them for animal-assisted therapy. But it was at the suggestion of a friend that Lainey decided to combine the goats' natural penchants for climbing and snuggling with the calm, positive vibes of yoga class. The result was incredible—goats and yoga were a perfect fit. Now, classes at the farm involve the "aid" of Lainey's goats—many of whom are rescues—as they clamber, nuzzle, and snuggle while participants stretch. And since starting, Lainey has welcomed even more goats onto her property, including baby goats like little Annie Goatley. Best of all, Goat Yoga has inspired classes all over the world. Not *baaa*d!

CAN CAMELS CRY?

Legend has it that the music ritual described in the column below (left) causes camels to weep with emotion. But many experts don't think so.

"Camels can activate their tear ducts to wash out their eyes if there's an irritant such as sand," says John Hare of the Wild Camel Protection Foundation. "They're crying for practical reasons, not emotional ones."

THE WEEPING CAMEL

GOBI DESERT, MONGOLIA

The baby camel's heartbreaking cry carried for miles on the desert wind. Botok the white Bactrian camel had been rejected by his mother, who ignored the calf every time he came near her. Now Botok was starved for milk and attention. The concerned owners, a family of nomadic herders, were worried the calf would die.

The family sent their two sons, Dude and Ugna, across the desert on other camels to ask for the help of a violinist. They hoped an age-old music ritual would reunite the mother and baby camel. As the musician played his *morin khuur* (MOO-rin HOOR), or horse-head fiddle, another person sang and stroked the mother camel's wool.

Amazingly, the mother camel nuzzled Botok and allowed him to nurse. Her eyes filled with tears. The baby was saved! It seems that the ritual worked, and the camels were a family once again.

ROCK STAR

OURAY, COLORADO, U.S.A.

Biskit the Jack Russell terrier is definitely not afraid of heights. She goes rock climbing with her owner! Pulling herself up with powerful little toes and squeezing her muscle-toned body through crevices, Biskit has made dozens of climbs—some higher than 600 feet. Owner Tom Kelly says she seems to be able to sniff out the best routes to get to the top the fastest. "Biskit is like a little goat," Kelly says. "She'll climb some rocks that people can't even manage." And if she doesn't feel like climbing mountains, she'll climb trees to chase squirrels!

Jack Russells are energetic and athletic by nature.

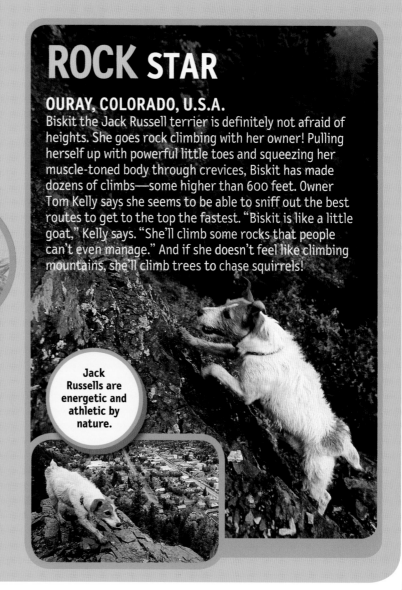

FOLLOWING THE HERD

Male bison may weigh a ton—literally—but don't let their size fool you; these big guys can stampede at speeds of about 35 miles an hour.

1 "We are so bored."

2 "Yahoo!!!!"

3 "Hey, guys! Same place next week!"

BALTIMORE, MARYLAND, U.S.A.

Police may know how to arrest criminals, but these officers were scratching their heads when they had to capture some odd fugitives: a herd of bison! Nine woolly animals escaped from a farm early one morning and invaded a nearby neighborhood. Police arrived to find the massive mammals shuffling across front lawns as startled homeowners looked on. Linking hands to form a human chain, the officers herded the animals onto an empty tennis court. Some bison even started leaping over the net! "For such big animals, they moved pretty gracefully," says Officer Shawn Vinson. Finally, police officers and local farmhands guided the bison into an animal trailer using deck chairs and mesh fencing. Why did they leave the farm in the first place? "One of them probably got out," Vinson says, "and the rest just followed!"

BIG CAT CAUGHT ON CAMERA

HOLLYWOOD, CALIFORNIA, U.S.A.

Meet P-22, the mountain lion unexpectedly *cata*pulted to fame. Unlike most California mountain lions that live in large areas of wilderness, P-22 settled in Los Angeles' urban Griffith Park, within view of the famous Hollywood sign. He was soon discovered when a remote wildlife camera snapped his picture. For his own safety, wildlife rangers carefully sedated the 120-pound (54-kg) cat, fitted him with a tracking collar, and then released him back into the wild. Soon, the big cat had attracted a fan following. He was featured in *National Geographic* magazine, and the city of Los Angeles even declared a day of recognition in his honor. Best of all, P-22's fame is raising awareness of mountain lions and the ways that people can peacefully coexist with them. P-22 sure is the cat's meow!

SNEAKY ELEPHANT DRAINS HOT TUB!

THIS SOUP IS ALL RIGHT, BUT IT COULD USE A LITTLE SALT.

MADIKWE GAME RESERVE, SOUTH AFRICA

Susan Potgieter was stumped. At night, the hot tubs at Etali Safari Lodge were full of water, but by morning they had drained to almost nothing. Potgieter, the lodge's owner, found no leaks or cracks. Finally, the culprit was caught in the act: An elephant was drinking from the hot tub.

Troublesome—nicknamed after the incident—got caught, but it turns out many of the reserve's 400 elephants used the hot tubs like watering holes. "Some elephants like warmer water, especially when it's chilly outside," Potgieter says. "The hot tubs were an easy way for them to get a clean, warm drink."

Nowadays the hot tubs are surrounded by harmless electric fences to encourage the elephants to use natural sources. But guests have other naughty wild animals to deal with. "Birds will see their reflections in the guests' windows," Potgieter says. "Early in the morning they'll squawk at the 'other bird' and wake everyone up!"

STORKS IN LOVE

BASEL, SWITZERLAND

Some might call this a true love story: Despite being away for more than six months every year, Romeo the stork always returns to the same zoo. Why? Because that's where his nest is—and where Julia the stork lives.

Male storks often fly back to the same nest every year and wait for a female to arrive to mate. But when Julia broke her wing three years ago, she wasn't able to migrate like other wild storks and permanently moved into the zoo. Romeo can't seem to live without her and returns around the end of March, probably from Africa. The result? The couple hatches about three or four chicks each summer. "Once Romeo arrives, she throws her head back and makes a sound with her beak, like clapping," says zoo curator Friederike von Houwald. Happy Valentine's Day, Romeo and Julia!

The legend about storks bringing babies to parents may have started because of storks' habit of returning to the same nests each year, giving them reputations for being devoted parents.

When Wiggles and the puppies started to eat solid food, Wiggles would eat only puppy chow instead of her special pig food.

PUPPY HOG

RANTOUL, KANSAS, U.S.A.

Wiggles the pig may actually think of herself as top dog! Born a runt, Wiggles was too small to stay with her birth mom and about a dozen siblings. So she slept in a playpen with a litter of puppies that had just been born to Clementine, the terrier mix. Soon the pig became one of the family—the dog family, that is. "Wiggles wrestled and played with the other puppies, and they'd all sleep in a pile at night," says Nellie Davis, who owns Clementine. "And she'd kind of nibble on us like a puppy would." Wiggles even nursed alongside her adopted puppy siblings, drinking milk from Clementine. Years later, Wiggles still recognized her doggie mom. But Clementine kept her distance: Wiggles grew to more than 300 pounds!

GRUMPY CAT
GETS FAMOUS

MORRISTOWN, ARIZONA, U.S.A.
This cat may look grumpy, but she's *feline* fine. Grumpy Cat, whose real name is Tardar Sauce, is world famous for her trademark frown and cranky messages. Her unique look and adorable attitude have earned her a fortune and millions of fans, including more than two million followers on social media. Although her mother was a standard domestic shorthair, Grumpy Cat's permanent pout and short stature were likely caused by a genetic mutation called dwarfism. And while she may *look* upset, there are actually two things that make Grumpy Cat very happy: being held and being petted by her owner.

Grumpy Cat has a brother named Pokey.

I WISH THERE WERE ROOM FOR SOMEONE TO SIGN MY SPLINTS.

BUTTERFLY GETS SPLINTS

LAKE LUZERNE, NEW YORK, U.S.A.
The monarch butterfly fluttered helplessly on the roadside. It had been hit by a car and broke its wing. Luckily, Jeannette Brandt spotted the creature while riding her bike and took it home.

Watching a how-to video, Brandt glued two tiny cardboard splints over the monarch's broken wing. For ten days, Brandt fed the butterfly water and mushy pear. "It ate off my hand," she says. "It seemed grateful for the help."

But one challenge remained: migration. "Monarchs winter in Mexico each year," says Chris Singer, founder of the Live Monarch Foundation. But Mexico was 3,000 miles away from New York, and it was now too cold for the butterfly to begin its journey. So nestled in a shoebox, the butterfly hitched a ride with a southbound trucker. The trucker released it in Florida, where, perhaps with a wave of its splinted wing, the small survivor took flight.

Orangutans build sleeping platforms in trees using branches, twigs, and leaves.

CAMP LEAKEY, TANJUNG PUTING RESERVE, BORNEO

Keep an eye on your vessel when Princess the orangutan is around. The boatnapping buccaneer stole canoes from the dock at the research station where she lives! Princess took the boats so she could get to the tasty plants that grow downstream. But she may have had another motive: "If there were people around, sometimes she would do it to show off," said scientist Biruté Mary Galdikas, Camp Leakey's orangutan expert.

Princess's rides could be a royal pain for camp workers, who had to retrieve the canoes she abandoned. To discourage her, they stored the canoes underwater. But Princess simply tipped the boats from side to side until the water sloshed out.

All primates are intelligent, but Princess is especially brainy. "I'd say she's one of the smartest orangutans I've ever seen in my life," Galdikas says. Even when Princess is on shore, she eats like a queen: She figured out how to use a key to unlock the camp's dining hall!

APE TAKES BOAT FOR A RIDE!

Goldie, an ostrich like the one at right, tried to cross the Golden Gate Bridge when she came to it.

OSTRICH ESCAPES!

SAN FRANCISCO, CALIFORNIA, U.S.A.

Goldie the ostrich tied up traffic when she went sightseeing—in the middle of the Golden Gate Bridge! Owner Ron Love was carting Goldie and another ostrich across the bridge in a van when he heard the sound of breaking glass. Seeing feathers floating in his side-view mirror, he realized Goldie had accidentally knocked out one of the windows—and harmlessly squeezed herself out onto the bridge! "She's six feet tall," Love says. "I don't know how she fit through the window!" Traffic screeched to a halt as locals and tourists alike watched Goldie race around the roadway. About four minutes later, police cars on the scene formed a barrier so Love could herd the bird off the bridge. Now she's safe and sound on Love's farm—and will never have to cross a busy bridge again!

> Ostriches can run almost as fast as the Golden Gate Bridge's 45-mile-an-hour (72 km/h) speed limit.

DOG RESCUES BABY

NAIROBI, KENYA, AFRICA

An abandoned baby girl lay in the forest, wrapped in an old pair of shorts. Weak and hungry, the helpless infant didn't have much chance of survival—until a stray pooch called Doggie came along.

With her mouth, Doggie gently dragged the bundle across a busy road, right up to a gate. "She probably dragged the baby about 300 yards," says Jean Gilchrist of the Kenya Society for the Protection and Care of Animals. Children heard the baby's cries, and their mother came to help.

"The baby would have died if she had been left in the forest," Gilchrist says. But thanks to Doggie and some intensive nursing, the girl is now healthy. After the rescue, the press dubbed Doggie *Mkombozi*, which means "savior" in Swahili, an African language. That's a fitting name for this four-footed hero.

Doggie and the baby were adopted by loving people.

YES, DEER!

WIESBADEN, GERMANY

Mädchen the German shepherd mix didn't mind fawning all over her new friend. Maybe it was because her new friend was a baby deer! Animal control officers brought the orphaned fawn to Lydia Weber, who was known for adopting animals. But it was her dog who really took over the mothering. Mädchen started by licking the deer—now called Mausi—from head to toe. And when Mausi wouldn't drink milk from a bottle, Weber held the bottle under Mädchen so that the fawn would feel like it was nursing from its mother. No matter what, Mausi's bond to her doggie mom will always be "en-deer-ing"!

PIG PAINTS PICTURES

CAPE TOWN, SOUTH AFRICA

Some people think of pigs as dirty, unintelligent animals. But not only are they smart, clean creatures, it turns out that they are also artistic! Pigcasso was rescued by her owner, Joanne Lefson, in Cape Town, South Africa. Since pigs are such intelligent creatures, Joanne hoped to find a fun activity to keep Pigcasso from getting bored. And by using treats and a training tool called a clicker, Joanne was able to teach Pigcasso to paint! Pigcasso simply holds the brush in her mouth, dips it in paint, and gets to work creating masterpieces. Now, Pigcasso's artwork gets tons of attention. The paintings are even raising money for charity. So, how does someone know they've gotten hold of a Pigcasso original? She "signs" each piece with her noseprint.

Pigcasso's art may be delicate, but she weighs 450 pounds (204 kg).

Cubs like these got into a sticky situation!

MOUNTAIN LION TRACKS

Mountain lion cubs are blind for the first 10 days after birth.

BUTTE, MONTANA, U.S.A.

The railroad inspector's heart skipped a beat when he saw the three wet mountain lion cubs frozen to the icy-cold tracks. And a train was on its way!

After crossing a creek with their mother, the clumsy cubs—their paws and bellies dripping wet—had stuck fast when their wet bodies froze onto the steel rails. Thinking quickly, the inspector alerted oncoming trains to stop. Then he poured lukewarm coffee over the shivering cubs, trying to melt the ice that had formed on their paws. It didn't work. So state game warden Marty Vook tried a portable pump that squirted jets of warm water. Freedom!

"They scurried off into the bushes to their mama," Vook says. These cubs were very cool cats!

Casey Anderson plays with his best friend, Brutus.

MAKE SURE MY SALMON SMOOTHIE HAS A SLICE OF PINEAPPLE IN IT.

BEAR IS BEST FRIEND

BOZEMAN, MONTANA, U.S.A.

What do you call a bear that swims in your pool, eats at your table, and steals your hat? If you're Casey Anderson, you call him Brutus—and your best friend.

Anderson adopted the orphaned bear when Brutus was still small enough to fit in his hand. Growing up in Anderson's home, the cub would drink from baby bottles, sleep in a laundry basket, and sprawl out in front of the TV. When Brutus grew too big for the house, Anderson created Montana Grizzly Encounter, a three-acre bear sanctuary.

At the sanctuary, Anderson and Brutus educate visitors about how special bears are—and why they need to be protected in the wild. Brutus may be a teacher, but that doesn't mean he's not naughty. "We have a pond that feeds a waterfall through a pipe, and sometimes Brutus will put his paw over the pipe to stop the water," Anderson says. "When the other bears investigate, he takes his paw away and totally drenches them!"

Brutus and friends share dinner.

BEACH PARTY

CHINCOTEAGUE ISLAND, VIRGINIA, U.S.A.

An ocean channel seems like a weird place to find wild horses. But every year Chincoteague ponies have made the short swim from Assateague Island to Chincoteague Island. It's all part of Pony Penning, a fund-raiser for the local volunteer fire department. No one is quite sure why a herd of wild ponies lives on the island, now a wildlife refuge. Some believe that 17th-century settlers turned their horses loose. Today the spring foals are auctioned after they reach Chincoteague; the others swim back to Assateague. That's one big swim-a-thon!

In one year the Pony Penning raised about $120,000.

The first foal to reach shore is crowned King or Queen Neptune.

DOGS
GO SURFING

TOTALLY GNARLY!

DEL MAR, CALIFORNIA, U.S.A.

At a surfing contest in Del Mar, California, the contestants are experts at doggy paddling—because the surfers are all dogs! Held annually by a nonprofit animal rescue called the Helen Woodward Animal Center, the Surf Dog Surf-A-Thon lets pup participants catch waves instead of balls. Pooches of all shapes and sizes line up to "hang twenty," perching on special soft surfboards and riding the waves in to shore. Every dog wears a special life vest to stay safe. Participants can also join in on a costume contest, a dog agility course, and plenty of music, food, and fun. Plus, the event raises awareness and money for homeless animals. Totally rad!

Past events have raised more than $80,000 for homeless animals!

"Ears" to Zepo (front) and Bosco (center).

Servals and caracals can catch prey (usually birds and small mammals) by leaping into the air.

Servals are African wildcats weighing between 20 and 40 pounds. Caracals are found in Africa and Asia. They weigh between 29 and 42 pounds.

ONE COOL CAT

CEDAR, MINNESOTA, U.S.A.

Sometimes animals can be just as mean as people when it comes to accepting others who are considered "different." Zepo the wildcat didn't fit in when he first came to live at the Wild-cat Sanctuary. A serval and caracal mixed breed, Zepo looked different—and the other wildcats didn't like it. "The full-breed servals and caracals couldn't figure out what he was," director Tammy Quist says. "They would hiss at him and run away." An outcast, Zepo became sad and lonely.

Then came Bosco, a 12-week-old serval. Because he was a baby, the wildcat didn't know that Zepo was "different." Bosco just wanted a friend. Soon the two became inseparable, play-fully wrestling each other or sleeping curled up together. Zepo even sat outside Bosco's cage when the serval was recovering from surgery. And what do you think happened when Bosco, who was popular with the servals and caracals, introduced his friend to the other wildcats? They accepted Zepo, too! Maybe they learned what all party animals know: the more, the merrier!

LLAMA LOVES TO LEAP

PORTHMADOG, WALES, UK

When Caspa the two-year-old llama arrived at Black Rock Llama Center in Porthmadog, Wales, all he seemed to do was spit, kick, and nip at unguarded ankles. He also refused to go near his owner, Sue Williams. Instead, he played elaborate games of tag that sometimes lasted days! Sue refused to give up, though, and decided to give Caspa a different game to play: she set up an agility course similar to the kind dogs use, and led Caspa through it. Over a short period, Caspa reached new heights—literally. He became a leaping llama, regularly clearing hurdles over three feet (1 m) high. In fact, the frisky flier even broke a world record: At an agility show, he cleared a jump of 3 feet 8.5 inches (1.13 m). And best of all, Caspa transformed into a happy "highflier."

BADGER BREAK-IN!

WILTSHIRE COUNTY, ENGLAND, U.K.

Everyone's heard of prison breakouts—but two British badgers managed to pull off a prison break-*in!*

The badgers evaded Erlestoke Prison authorities for weeks while they ate their fill of earthworms from the prison lawn. They even stumped officials as to how they broke in. Badgers usually dig underground tunnels with their strong claws. But the fence around the prison goes deep into the ground, so the furry fugitives probably had to squeeze through the front gates.

The badgers might have decided to become jailbirds because of the prison yard's quiet location and large supply of earthworms. "The prisoners would also throw food out the windows to them," says Malcolm Clark of the Wiltshire Badger Group.

After several failed attempts, authorities finally captured the badgers and forced them to freedom. Let's hope the critters don't become repeat offenders.

The prison

ERLESTOKE

Badgers like the two above staged a break-in at Erlestoke Prison.

> A badger can eat several hundred earthworms in a night.

CAT CALLS COPS

> I'M READY FOR MY HEROISM MEDAL.

COLUMBUS, OHIO, U.S.A.

When Gary Rosheisen rescued Tommy the cat from a shelter, he didn't know that three years later Tommy would rescue *him*.

One afternoon while trying to move from his wheelchair to his bed, Rosheisen slipped and fell on the floor. He yelled for help, but no one heard him—and the phone was out of reach. Cold and sore, Rosheisen thought he'd be stuck on the floor until his nurse arrived the next day.

But ten minutes later, a police officer came to Rosheisen's apartment and said a 911 call had been placed from his phone. Rosheisen said that was impossible—until he remembered that several months earlier, he had tried to train Tommy to push the 911 button. "I told the policeman about it. He went into the living room and there was Tommy, right by the phone."

Did Tommy mean to dial 911? "You could certainly train a cat to dial the phone," animal trainer Roland Sonnenburg says. "I'm not sure he understood calling 911 would help his owner, but I won't say it's impossible." Whether Tommy's fancy footwork was intentional or just lucky, Rosheisen is grateful he has a cat that's quick on the dial.

> About 40 out of every 100 cats favor their left front paws over their right. Around 40 favor both front paws, and only 20 favor their right.

Natumi, page 18

Index

Index

Credits

Credits

Prepared by the Book Division
Hector Sierra, *Senior Vice President and General Manager*
Nancy Laties Feresten, *Senior Vice President, Editor in Chief, Children's Books*
Jonathan Halling, *Design Director, Books and Children's Publishing*
Jay Sumner, *Director of Photography, Children's Publishing*
Jennifer Emmett, *Editorial Director, Children's Books*
Eva Absher-Schantz, *Managing Art Director, Children's Books*
Carl Mehler, *Director of Maps*
R. Gary Colbert, *Production Director*
Jennifer A. Thornton, *Director of Managing Editorial*

Staff for This Book
Robin Terry, *Project Editor*
Kelley Miller, *Illustrations Editor*
James Hiscott, Jr., *Art Director*
Grace Hill, *Associate Managing Editor*
Joan Gossett, *Production Editor*
Lewis R. Bassford, *Production Manager*
Susan Borke, *Legal and Business Affairs*
Kate Olesin, *Assistant Editor*
Kathryn Robbins, *Design Production Assistant*
Hillary Moloney, *Illustrations Assistant*
Jean Mendoza, Catherine Monson, *Editorial Interns*

Manufacturing and Quality Management
Christopher A. Liedel, *Chief Financial Officer*
Phillip L. Schlosser, *Senior Vice President*
Chris Brown, *Technical Director*
Nicole Elliott, *Manager*
Rachel Faulise, *Manager*
Robert L. Barr, *Manager*

Based on the "Amazing Animals" department in *National Geographic Kids* magazine
Rachel Buchholz, *Executive Editor*
Andrea Silen, *Associate Editor*
Margaret J. Krauss, *Assistant Editor*
Sharon Thompson, *Copy Editor*
Kelley Miller, *Senior Photo Editor*
Nicole Lazarus, *Art Director*
Stewart Bean, *Digital Design Assistant*

Since 1888, the National Geographic Society has funded more than 12,000 research, exploration, and preservation projects around the world. The Society receives funds from National Geographic Partners, LLC, funded in part by your purchase. A portion of the proceeds from this book supports this vital work. To learn more, visit natgeo.com/info.

NATIONAL GEOGRAPHIC and Yellow Border Design are trademarks of the National Geographic Society, used under license.

For more information, please visit nationalgeographic.com, call 1-800-647-5463, or write to the following address:
National Geographic Partners
1145 17th Street N.W.
Washington, D.C. 20036-4688 U.S.A.

Visit us online at nationalgeographic.com/books
For librarians and teachers: ngchildrensbooks.org
More for kids from National Geographic: natgeokids.com

For information about special discounts for bulk purchases, please contact National Geographic Books Special Sales: specialsales@natgeo.com

For rights or permissions inquiries, please contact National Geographic Books Subsidiary Rights: bookrights@natgeo.com

Trade paperback ISBN: 978-1-4263-0918-2
Reinforced library edition ISBN: 978-1-4263-0919-9

Printed in China
19/RRDH/9 (PB)
19/RRDH/6 (RLB)

Contributing Writers: Allie Benjamin, Lynn Brunelle, Christina Chan, Laura Daily, Elisabeth Deffner, Madaline Donnelly, Scott Elder, Sara Fleetwood, Sarah Wassner Flynn, Jacqueline Geschickter, Gail Skroback Hennessey, Kristin Hunt, Marinell James, Kitson Jazynka, Jamie Kiffel-Alchem, Karen Kraft, Stefan Lovgren, Adrienne Mason, Ruth A. Musgrave, Aline Alexander Newman, Carolyn Patek, Amanda Pressner, Kristin Baird Rattini, Johnna Rizzo, Amanda Sandlin, Heather E. Schwartz, B.F. Summers, C.M. Tomlin, Pamela S. Turner, Deborah K. Underwood, Erin Whitmer, Diane Williamson, MaryAlice Yakutchik